Love to Anna
On your 28th Birthday
From Mum & Dad
xx

Jane Packer's Complete Guide To
Flower Arranging

JANE PACKER'S COMPLETE GUIDE TO
FLOWER ARRANGING

DORLING KINDERSLEY
LONDON · NEW YORK · STUTTGART

A DORLING KINDERSLEY BOOK

Photography
Dave King

Project Editor
Stefanie Foster

Art Editor
Tracey Clarke

Editorial Assistant
Nell Graville

Designer
Helen Diplock

D.T.P. Designer
Karen Ruane

Senior Editor
Susannah Marriott

Managing Editor
Rosie Pearson

Managing Art Editor
Carole Ash

Production Manager
Maryann Rogers

*Dedicated to my wonderful family for all that they do,
especially Gary, Rebby and my little Lola*

First published in Great Britain in 1995
by Dorling Kindersley Limited,
9 Henrietta Street, London WC2E 8PS

A CIP catalogue record for this book is available
from the British Library

ISBN 0 7513 0169 8

Reproduced in Italy by GRB Editrice, Verona
Printed and bound in Italy by A. Mondadori Editore, Verona

CONTENTS

INTRODUCTION

I HAVE SPENT ALL MY WORKING DAYS with flowers, and feel fortunate to be surrounded by their beauty and freshness most of the time. I began working in a florist's shop at the age of 15 as a Saturday girl, and what started as means to earn a bit of pocket money developed into a fascination with and life-long love of flowers. I couldn't believe what could be done with flowers, and how much detail, passion and hard work was involved in their preparation.

In this small shop in a small town, during an era in which most people would never consider buying flowers for themselves, floral arrangements were sold mainly for birthdays, anniversaries, weddings and, ultimately, funerals – the major milestones in life. Today, things are different, people **do** buy flowers solely for themselves, and on a regular basis, too. Supermarkets have started to include flowers within their range of essential produce, making them more accessible to most people, and although the current range of flowers they offer may sometimes be limited, it is growing rapidly. And with an ever-increasing selection of blooms and foliage available, the hunger for whatever the "new look" may be is constantly growing, too.

During my career I have worked in all areas of the flower industry, and I have often found a reticence among my colleagues to share their skills and information with the general public. Some florists feel that by selling florist's foam to customers and showing them how to arrange flowers, they may endanger their own livelihood. I believe this attitude is wrong. To encourage people to arrange flowers more often and to experiment with and enjoy the myriad varieties available means they will buy more flowers, demand different varieties, and expect longer lasting and better-conditioned blooms. This has to be good both for the flower industry – an industry I feel passionately about – and for the pleasure people derive from flowers. In 1989 I opened a school of flower arranging in London. Since its beginning, I have met many people who have a wonderful eye for colour and a real love of flowers, but who are desperate for more information and guidance on what to do with flowers. They long to escape from the rigid, formal teaching that many have experienced with traditional exponents of "floral art", toward a more day-to-day and realistic approach. They come to my school because they want to achieve with flowers a look that is natural, uncontrived and easy to live with. These ideas embody my philosophy of flower arranging and I have aimed to demonstrate them in this book.

There have been many beautiful inspirational books published on the subject of flowers and there will, of course, be many more in the future. What I believe this book can offer is a precise insight into how to choose flowers and work with them. From a simple posy to the trickiest bridal shower bouquet, I have tried to explain the mysteries involved with simple instructions and clear step-by-step photographs. I hope these practical projects will improve your flower arranging technique and inspire you to experiment with your own ideas.

Jane Packer

THE PRINCIPLES OF FLOWER ARRANGING

The inherent properties of the flowers and foliage you decide to use should always set the style of an arrangement, establishing its dominant colour, shape and texture. While traditional flower-arranging techniques provide useful guidelines, I do not consider them as rigid rules. It is far more important to express yourself and create a display that sits comfortably in its setting.

STYLES OF ARRANGEMENT

WHEN STARTING an arrangement, consider whether the eventual setting of the display calls for a formal, modern or casual theme. Then think about the container you plan to use, and which flowers will enhance its size, shape, colour and texture. Here, all the containers are made of galvanized metal, but each one has a distinct style and will be displayed in a different setting, so the results look quite diverse.

POTTED DISPLAY
Planted arrangements are most striking when kept simple. A single ornamental cabbage needs no adornment to create impact in a simple galvanized jug and suits a variety of settings.

CLASSIC FORMAL DISPLAY
Strong lines and a sparing use of flowers suit a clean, formal setting. These roses impart classic grace to a tall vase with a suitably sharp outline.

COUNTRY-STYLE ARRANGEMENT
*A random variety of red and orange flowers
and foliage presents a casual, unstudied
display in a country-style jug, perfect for
an informal location.*

MODERN GROUPED ARRANGEMENT
*Small unusual containers grouped together
and filled with one type of flower make a
stylish, innovative arrangement for a
contemporary backdrop. Here, the containers
are as important a feature as the flowers.*

DRIED MAIZE COBS form the backbone of the arrangement

FLOWERS AND PLANT MATERIAL are massed in groups by type

SMALL TERRACOTTA POTS are secured by pushing a cut stem from one of the plants through the base into the dry foam

THICK MAIZE COB STEMS are cut on a slant to make them easier to push into the dry foam

LARGE INFORMAL DRIED ARRANGEMENT
The lack of movement and suppleness in dried flowers means they risk appearing stiff and spiky if used sparingly. To avoid this, mass the flowers together by type, keeping the arrangement compact and bold. Massing flowers in groups not only intensifies their colours and exaggerates textural contrasts, but also recreates the way they grow naturally, which is particularly appropriate for a casual setting.

DEEP PURPLE LARKSPUR lift the arrangement, contrasting vividly with the rich yellow sunflower heads

GNARLED SUNFLOWER LEAVES, saved from the stem, provide interesting textural contrast

LOW TERRACOTTA BOWL packed with dry foam

LARGER STALKS OF TIMOTHY hang over the edge of the container

CHOOSING FRESH FLOWERS

FRESH FLOWERS TRANSFORM A ROOM with their beauty, colour and scent. Select stems partly in bud to last longer, and, if combining flowers, try to mix varieties of similar longevity. Bold, eye-catching flowers provide the focal point for an arrangement, while less conspicuous blooms act as filler and recessionary material.

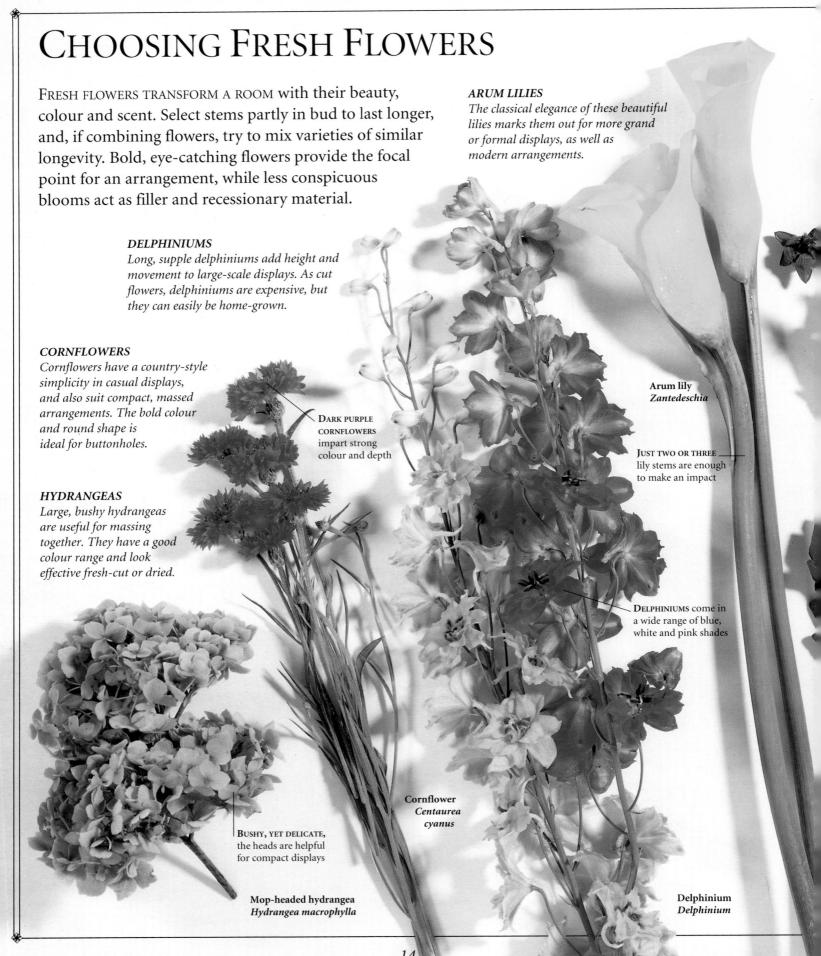

ARUM LILIES
The classical elegance of these beautiful lilies marks them out for more grand or formal displays, as well as modern arrangements.

DELPHINIUMS
Long, supple delphiniums add height and movement to large-scale displays. As cut flowers, delphiniums are expensive, but they can easily be home-grown.

CORNFLOWERS
Cornflowers have a country-style simplicity in casual displays, and also suit compact, massed arrangements. The bold colour and round shape is ideal for buttonholes.

DARK PURPLE CORNFLOWERS impart strong colour and depth

HYDRANGEAS
Large, bushy hydrangeas are useful for massing together. They have a good colour range and look effective fresh-cut or dried.

Arum lily
Zantedeschia

JUST TWO OR THREE lily stems are enough to make an impact

DELPHINIUMS come in a wide range of blue, white and pink shades

BUSHY, YET DELICATE, the heads are helpful for compact displays

Cornflower
Centaurea cyanus

Mop-headed hydrangea
Hydrangea macrophylla

Delphinium
Delphinium

DAHLIAS
*Lush dahlias make a strong
statement when mixed together
in a display of clashing colours.*

PREVENT SILKY BLOOMS
from drooping by adding
flower food to the water

ROSES
*The beauty, scent and romance of
roses make them the most popular
of fresh flowers. Choose blooms
that are not yet fully open.*

ASTILBE
*Light, feathery astilbe form
the perfect complement to
heavier flowers. They
range in colour from
cream and pink
to dark red.*

THE STRONG SHAPES
and bold colours of
dahlias make for a
good focal point

ASTILBE should be
used in combined
displays as a foil for
heavier flowers

Pink
Dianthus

WAXY, DARK ROSE
LEAVES – a good choice
for filler foliage

Dahlia
Dahlia

Rose
Rosa

Astilbe
Astilbe

PINKS
*Traditional and
long-lasting, pinks
are smaller than
carnations. They have
a sweet scent and suit table
displays and buttonholes.*

ENCOURAGE NEW BUDS
to open by removing
old flower heads

CHOOSING FOLIAGE

ALMOST EVERY ARRANGEMENT includes foliage, whether on the flowers themselves, or as a separate ingredient. Foliage is used in displays as filler material, or to add textural and colour contrast. Stronger, bold pieces can be used to form the outline of an arrangement, while longer, supple foliage adds width and a sense of movement.

IVY
A popular, year-round foliage, ivy softens any display with its trailing lines. A wide range of leaf sizes comes in plain green and variegated patterns.

ROSEMARY
Supple lengths of rosemary spill out effectively from a display, while short stems are good fillers.

PLANTAIN LILIES
A smooth surface and strong leaf shape make this variety of hosta ideal for the base of displays, or as edging to larger bunches.

EUCALYPTUS
An extremely versatile type of foliage, eucalyptus in its many varieties works as beautiful filler material for all sorts of arrangements.

FLOWER HEADS add movement and highlights of colour

FLAT, SMOOTH LEAVES complement larger, defined flowers

ROSEMARY provides a delicious scent and silvery tones

TENDRILS OF IVY impart a flowing quality to arrangements

Eucalyptus
Eucalyptus

Ivy
Hedera

Plantain lily
Hosta fortunei
'Aureomarginata'

Rosemary
Rosmarinus officinalis

BUPLEURUM

This country-looking foliage is a pleasing filler that provides colour contrast with its soft lime-green flowers.

Shrubby hare's ear, Bupleurum *Bupleurum*

BEAR GRASS

A fine classical foliage, this grass is best used sparingly with architectural flowers such as lilies and amaryllis for a modern, minimalist feel.

Bear grass *Dasylirion*

STRONG, FLEXIBLE STEMS add flowing lines and minimalist elegance to simple displays

BUTCHER'S BROOM

There are several different types of Ruscus, *and they all last up to four weeks. The variety featured here lends a soft, arching quality to taller displays.*

Butcher's broom *Ruscus aculeatus*

SMOOTH, SHINY supple stems create a strong structure

COPPER BEECH

A summer foliage, copper beech should not be used too early in the season as its new leaves are soft and wilt quickly. The strong copper colour is a valuable alternative to green foliage.

DARK MAHOGANY LEAVES are useful for colour contrast and as filler foliage

Copper beech *Fagus sylvatica* 'Cuprea'

CHOOSING DRIED FLOWERS

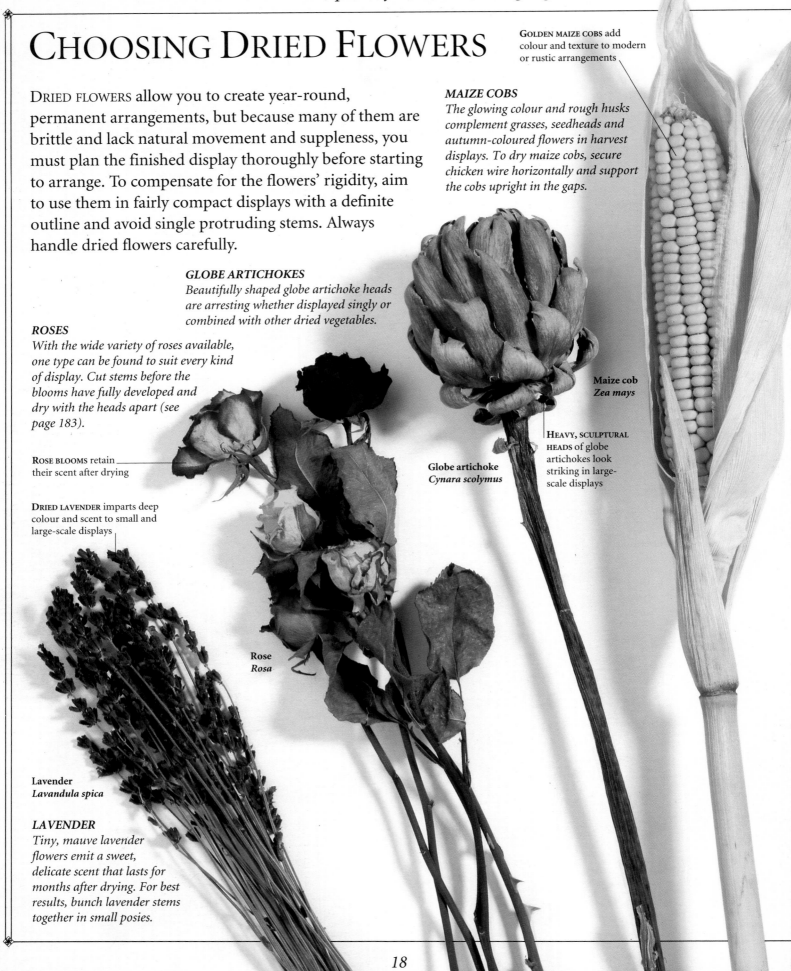

DRIED FLOWERS allow you to create year-round, permanent arrangements, but because many of them are brittle and lack natural movement and suppleness, you must plan the finished display thoroughly before starting to arrange. To compensate for the flowers' rigidity, aim to use them in fairly compact displays with a definite outline and avoid single protruding stems. Always handle dried flowers carefully.

GOLDEN MAIZE COBS add colour and texture to modern or rustic arrangements

MAIZE COBS
The glowing colour and rough husks complement grasses, seedheads and autumn-coloured flowers in harvest displays. To dry maize cobs, secure chicken wire horizontally and support the cobs upright in the gaps.

GLOBE ARTICHOKES
Beautifully shaped globe artichoke heads are arresting whether displayed singly or combined with other dried vegetables.

ROSES
With the wide variety of roses available, one type can be found to suit every kind of display. Cut stems before the blooms have fully developed and dry with the heads apart (see page 183).

ROSE BLOOMS retain their scent after drying

DRIED LAVENDER imparts deep colour and scent to small and large-scale displays

Maize cob
Zea mays

HEAVY, SCULPTURAL HEADS of globe artichokes look striking in large-scale displays

Globe artichoke
Cynara scolymus

Rose
Rosa

Lavender
Lavandula spica

LAVENDER
Tiny, mauve lavender flowers emit a sweet, delicate scent that lasts for months after drying. For best results, bunch lavender stems together in small posies.

Choosing Dried Flowers

SUNFLOWERS

The size and colour of sunflowers suit them both to sophisticated and country-style displays. The flowers can be massed, either on the stems or cut down, and the leaves also provide interesting dried foliage.

THE BOLD, CHEERFUL COLOUR and distinct shape of sunflowers make them a dramatic focal point flower

Sunflower
Helianthus

AMARANTHUS

The supple stems of fresh amaranthus become poker-straight when dried. Its lime-green and rusty red flowers impart warmth and texture to summer and autumn displays.

POPPY SEEDHEADS

Oval-shaped and smooth-surfaced, poppy seedheads combine well with richly coloured flowers and foliage. Spray-paint the heads for use in more festive displays.

Poppy seedhead
Papaver

SMOOTH, MAUVE-GREY poppy seedheads give structure and a distinctive shape to many types of display

VIBRANT-COLOURED circular heads are available in a wide spectrum of colours

VELVETY SPIRES soften textural arrangements

Amaranthus
Amaranthus

Strawflower
Helichrysum bracteatum

STRAWFLOWERS

The compact, rounded heads of strawflowers look striking when massed together. They have weak stems, so often need to be wired.

COLOUR SCHEMES

COLOUR IS THE PREDOMINANT FACTOR in any arrangement, and while the style of display and range of flower forms play an equal part in the finished piece, colour makes the initial impression. It is important to experiment with different tones, and to mix and match shades. Do not be afraid of testing new colour combinations – even traditional "clashes" of colour can look impressively vibrant.

BOLD RED DAHLIAS impart a rich opulence

RIBBON is used to pick out the colour of the dahlias

DEEP BLUE DELPHINIUMS contribute depth

PURE YELLOW ROSES have a vibrant, luminous quality

PRIMARY COLOURS
Bringing the primary colours on the colour wheel – blue, red and yellow – together in an arrangement creates a strong colour scheme. By just softening each tone the overall effect would be more subtle.

MAUVE SCABIOUS form a link between the lilac-coloured delphiniums and purple cornflowers

LILAC DELPHINIUMS are a lighter shade of the primary blue colour

VIOLET LISIANTHUS complement the primary vibrant yellow of arum lilies and marigolds

MONOCHROMATIC SCHEMES
A monochromatic colour scheme uses shades of the same colour. Here, a range of blues, including both strong and delicate shades, forms a harmonious blend.

COMPLEMENTARY COMBINATIONS
In the colour wheel, each secondary colour is the complement of the one primary not used in its make-up, and combining the two can look striking. Here, violet (formed from red and blue) is mixed with its missing primary, yellow.

BALANCING CONTAINERS AND FLOWERS

THE CONTAINER IS INTEGRAL TO THE DESIGN of a flower display, and its size, shape, colour and texture all affect the choice of flowers, and determine the final effect. When container and flowers are sympathetic to one another, the display is seen as one object. Clear glass containers almost disappear in a display, making them appropriate for most settings, while coloured or textured containers will always have a more significant influence over the choice of flowers and can be linked to their surroundings more emphatically.

LOW-LEVEL DISPLAY
Here, I have disregarded the traditional rule of using flowers at least twice the height of the container, but the compact group of full, round ranunculus complements the simple container perfectly.

MASSED FLOWERS
A massed group of delicate fairy-tale-like lachenalia sets off this squat, square tank, below right. Using one variety of flower en masse, rather than a mixture, presents a cleaner, bolder statement of modern simplicity.

CLASSICAL MODERNITY
Single stems of roses are ideal for the classic, clean look of this tall, cylindrical container. A display of this height should be viewed from the side, but larger, more open blooms could be cut quite short and placed in a low bowl display to be viewed from above.

RUSTIC JUG
A mixture of flowers and foliage clustered tightly together, below left, in a casual arrangement creates lots of natural charm. When grouped with the matching bowl, the containers form a lovely country composition.

NATURAL DISPLAY
This warm Provençal bowl intensifies and exaggerates the oranges in the flowers. The mixture of flowers, foliage and herbs suggests that they have been gathered and displayed on impulse.

ACID-GREEN EUPHORBIA breaks up the clashing reds, pinks and oranges of the flowers

THE CHOICE OF FROSTED GLASS transforms an essentially country-style display into something suitable for a modern setting

DRAMATIC CONTRAST

Flowers saturated with vibrant colour are a superb foil for this cool, frosted white bowl. Grouped in a random patchwork-like display, they spill over the bowl in a profusion of colour, their stylized extravagance echoed in the parrot tulips casually strewn alongside the bowl. The dramatic effect is enhanced by deliberately keeping the display as low as possible.

INTRICATELY FORMED rich pink parrot tulips contrast with the colour and texture of the bowl

HEAVIER BLOOMS HANG OVER the edge of the bowl, giving extra width to the display and a feeling of abundance

ARRANGING FRESH FLOWERS

Fresh flowers should not be confined to festivals or celebrations. The presence of flowers can subtly alter the atmosphere of a room, introducing a sense of calm and bringing natural freshness and colour indoors throughout the year. The projects that follow create different moods and encompass many styles of display, from a sophisticated table centre to a simple trug planted with spring bulbs.

ROUND TABLE DISPLAY
This luxurious arrangement uses a wide variety of flowers arranged by type to create a natural, informal look.

FOAM-BASED ARRANGEMENTS

EVERY ARRANGEMENT OF FRESH FLOWERS has its own unique style, often inspired by a special occasion, the decor and period of a room, or current fashion. Whether formal, homely or modern, the finished style can be as varied as the selection of flowers that make up the display, and florist's foam is invaluable in helping to create the effect you wish to achieve.

This traditional equipment is one of the conventions of floristry that I still use extensively. When soaked in water, it is ideal for creating natural-looking fresh flower arrangements in almost any shape or size of container. By supporting the flower stems and allowing them to draw off as much water as they need, the foam acts in much the same way as soil.

Balance of form is central to any successful arrangement, and florist's foam helps to achieve it, allowing you to place flowers so that the height of a display is proportionate to its width. The final position of an arrangement also affects its impact; foam enables you to angle the flower heads to suit a display viewed from above, placed against a wall or centred on a table. Flowers cut on a slant can also be easily positioned in foam to face in various directions and create gentle, curved outlines. This is useful when making front-facing displays and wreaths, or hiding a container behind trailing flowers and foliage.

Foam-based arrangements do not last as long as free-standing displays in fresh water, but you can prolong their life as much as possible by pushing stems toward the centre of the foam (taking care not to cross them) to prevent the foam from crumbling, and by topping up the water daily. To make sure the foam is thoroughly soaked, do not submerge it in water, but let it float on the surface. This allows the water to be absorbed all the way through the foam, and not just around the sides.

Front-facing Display
Page 30

Storm Lamp Ring
Page 36

Round Table Centre
Page 40

Basket Arrangement
Page 44

FRONT-FACING DISPLAY

WHEN MAKING A FRONT-FACING display, think of it as a "half-round" arrangement, aiming for soft curves and natural groupings of flowers. One common mistake is to position all the stems in one direction. Avoid this by ensuring some flowers lean backward. This prevents the display looking front-heavy and possibly falling forward.

DESIGN TIP
The display should be broadly triangular in shape but allow some longer stems to break the outline to soften the effect.

50cm (20in)

60cm (24in)

MATERIALS AND EQUIPMENT

If you wish, replace the flowers listed here with the same quantity of other flowers of a similar size and shape.

Flowers and foliage

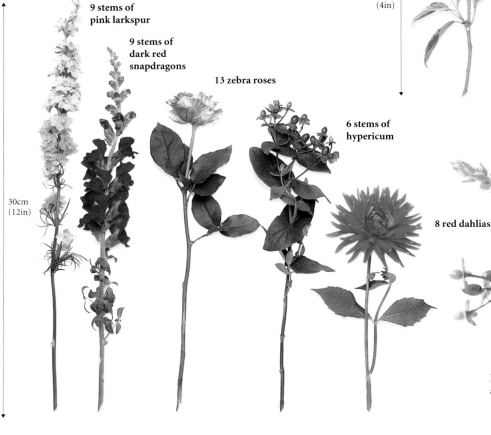

10 sprigs of variegated ivy

9 sprigs of maple

10cm (4in)

9 stems of pink larkspur

9 stems of dark red snapdragons

13 zebra roses

6 stems of hypericum

30cm (12in)

8 red dahlias

DARK RED DAHLIAS add depth

Container and equipment

Round bowl

9.5cm (3¾in)

20cm (8in)

Block of wet florist's foam taped to plastic saucer

12cm (4½in)

16cm (6½in)

PALE PINK LARKSPUR
set the height

DELICATE HYPERICUM BERRIES
fill in spaces

RED SNAPDRAGONS
continue the outline

SIDE VIEW
Create a full triangle with
some stems placed to fill
in the back of the display,
as shown.

THE FINISHED EFFECT
A rich and sumptuous
arrangement in toning
shades of red and pink,
backed by contrasting
light and dark foliage.

IVY AND MAPLE
provide filler
foliage

ZEBRA ROSES grouped
for a natural effect

MAKING THE DISPLAY

First prepare the flowers and foliage (see page 174).
Place the foam in the container up to about 2.5cm
(1in) higher than the rim. The techniques shown
here can be used for seasonal variations on the same
style of arrangement (see pages 34–35).

POSITION UPRIGHT
stems to fan out
slightly, and side stems
to point forward,
sideways, downward
and upward

GROUP STEMS in
threes for impact

ADD FLOWERS to the sides
and front in groups
of three

1 *Push stems of larkspur into the top of the
foam at the back, and into the sides, in groups
of three. Stems in each group should be of
different lengths. Angle the side stems downward,
and vertical stems slightly backward.*

2 *Add the snapdragons in
groups of three next to each group of
larkspur, at different lengths within each
group. Make sure they do not break the outline
created by the larkspur.*

PLACE THE ROSES centrally
and to the sides

3 *Add zebra roses as a focal point. Group
seven shorter-stemmed flowers deeper
and more centrally in the display, and
add three longer-stemmed roses to each side,
at different lengths and sloping downward.*

ZEBRA ROSES provide
the main focal point

Side view

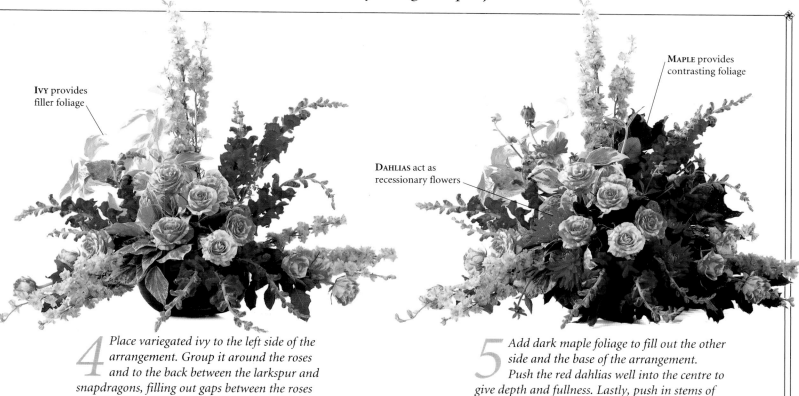

IVY provides filler foliage

MAPLE provides contrasting foliage

DAHLIAS act as recessionary flowers

4 Place variegated ivy to the left side of the arrangement. Group it around the roses and to the back between the larkspur and snapdragons, filling out gaps between the roses and the taller flowers.

5 Add dark maple foliage to fill out the other side and the base of the arrangement. Push the red dahlias well into the centre to give depth and fullness. Lastly, push in stems of hypericum berries to add the final delicate touch.

Alternative Colourway

You can transform the arrangement simply by varying the colour combination. Yellow roses and dill, replacing the pink roses, pick up the colours of the variegated ivy and change the emphasis.

Alternative flowers

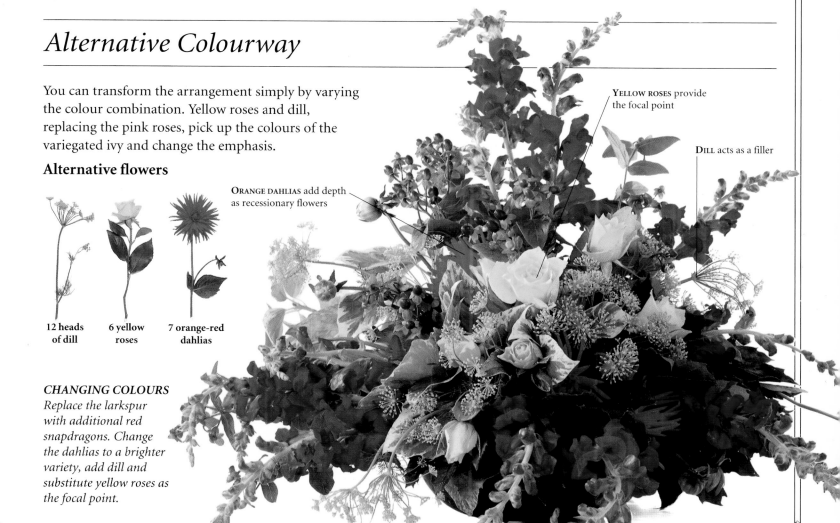

12 heads of dill

6 yellow roses

7 orange-red dahlias

ORANGE DAHLIAS add depth as recessionary flowers

YELLOW ROSES provide the focal point

DILL acts as a filler

CHANGING COLOURS
Replace the larkspur with additional red snapdragons. Change the dahlias to a brighter variety, add dill and substitute yellow roses as the focal point.

Winter Display

Adapt the principles used in the front-facing display on pages 30–33 to produce an opulent arrangement for mid-winter celebrations, such as Christmas. Leucadendron stems are pushed into the back and sides of wet florist's foam, followed by larger foliage, twigs and roses, arranged asymmetrically for a natural effect.

VARIEGATED HOLLY leaves provide filler foliage and soften the triangular outline

DELICATE RED SPRAY ROSES echo the colour of the larger crimson roses and add depth

BARK is pinned on to the florist's foam to start the arrangement

STEMS OF LEUCADENDRON set the height and width of the arrangement

VELVET-TEXTURED ROSES are placed through the centre of the display, providing the main focal point

DOGWOOD TWIGS break out of the triangular outline on both sides of the display

RUGGED BARK introduces a coarse texture and evokes the countryside

STORM LAMP RING

CREATING A RING OF FLOWERS around a central feature is an interesting exercise in floral design. Since candle-light, coupled with a rich array of flowers, is an ideal evening decoration, here I have chosen to work with a storm lamp. To maintain impact, ingredients are kept simple.

40cm (16in)

40cm (16in)

DESIGN TIP
Flowers and foliage are placed at three equidistant points around the ring, and the vibrant heads of achillea punctuate the circle of flowers and moss. This systematic approach ensures a well-balanced, yet natural-looking display.

MATERIALS AND EQUIPMENT

All flowers and foliage are pushed directly into the wet foam, and only the moss requires stub wires to hold it in place.

Flowers and foliage

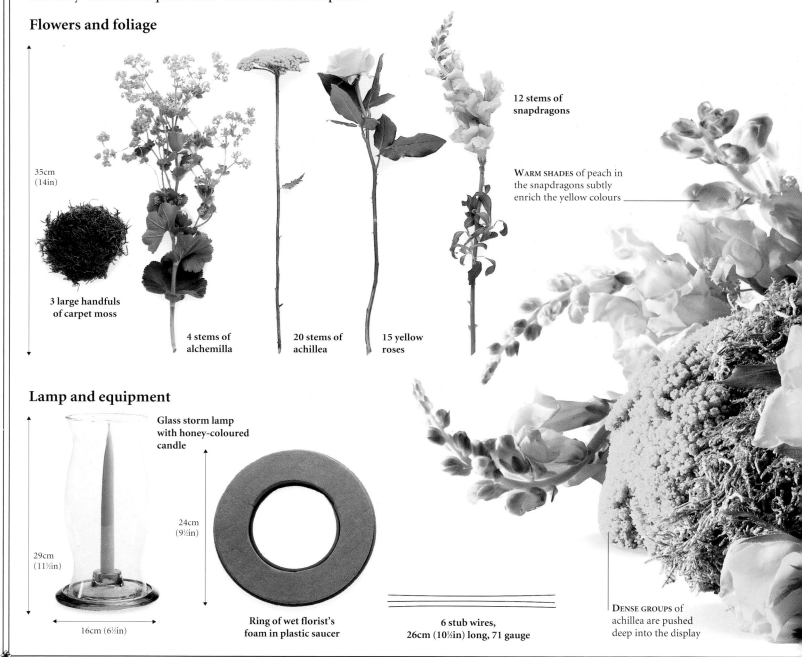

35cm (14in)

3 large handfuls of carpet moss

4 stems of alchemilla

20 stems of achillea

15 yellow roses

12 stems of snapdragons

WARM SHADES of peach in the snapdragons subtly enrich the yellow colours

DENSE GROUPS of achillea are pushed deep into the display

Lamp and equipment

Glass storm lamp with honey-coloured candle

24cm (9½in)

29cm (11½in)

16cm (6½in)

Ring of wet florist's foam in plastic saucer

6 stub wires, 26cm (10½in) long, 71 gauge

THE FINISHED EFFECT
*The natural curves of the snapdragon
stems add a sense of movement to an
otherwise compact arrangement.*

THE STORM LAMP
sets the height of
the decoration

SUPPLE SNAPDRAGONS
extend furthest from
the ring, contributing
movement to the display

YELLOW TIPS of alchemilla
are highlighted by the
vibrant yellows
surrounding them

ROSES are
the main
focal flower

MAKING THE RING

Foliage and flowers are attached in
groups on the wet foam ring. Each type
of material forms a separate group,
creating a compact, natural effect.

ATTACH THREE GROUPS
of moss at equal distances
around the ring

**ANGLE LONGER
LENGTHS** down
from the sides
and up toward
the lamp

*1 Put the storm lamp in the centre of the wet
foam ring in the saucer. Cut the stub wires
in half, bend into hairpin hooks (see page
177), and hook on the handfuls of moss at
three equally spaced points around the ring.*

*2 Cut shoots and leaves from the alchemilla
to 5–10cm (2–4in) in length. Push first the
leaves, then groups of buds into the foam
between the moss. Push shorter stems in deeper
and keep them in the centre of each group.*

*3 Trim the achillea stems to about 6cm
(2½in) and push them into the foam in
groups between the sections of moss and
alchemilla. Push the heads in deeper than the
alchemilla, keeping them level with the moss.*

KEEP THE ACHILLEA
flower heads level
with the moss

PUSH IN THE ACHILLEA
on either side of
the moss

4 *Cut the leaves off the roses and trim the stems to 5cm (2in). Divide the leaves into three separate groups, then the heads. Push groups of leaves, then flowers between the alchemilla and moss. Finally, trim the snapdragons to 15cm (6in). Add in three groups around the ring.*

MAKE SURE the roses stand out above the achillea, but are below the level of the alchemilla

LET LONGER LEAVES extend from the base of the ring

Alternative Colourway

The mood has been changed here by substituting subtly tinted flowers for warm, sunny yellows and by selecting a pastel green candle.

Alternative flowers and foliage

6 mauve mop-headed hydrangeas

12 shoots of senecio

15 stems of lisianthus

MOP-HEADED HYDRANGEAS replace the achillea

TRAILING SENECIO takes the place of the snapdragons

FRESH TONES
Purple-tipped lisianthus, mop-headed hydrangeas, and senecio replace the roses, achillea and snapdragons respectively. A muted green candle complements these new colours, and the overall effect is more delicate.

LISIANTHUS FLOWERS are substituted for roses

ROUND TABLE CENTRE

USING TRADITIONAL FLOWER-ARRANGING techniques, I have arranged flowers and foliage symmetrically to build up a display on foam that gives the impression of a posy. Vibrant orange poppies and tulips are grouped by type, their bold shapes and colour softened by delicate narcissi and bushy hebe.

40cm (16in)

60cm (24in)

DESIGN TIP
While the arrangement is round, it looks triangular from the side. Twigs, flowers and foliage are pushed into the florist's foam in equally spaced groups around the sides, establishing the circular shape and overall symmetry.

MATERIALS AND EQUIPMENT
No special container is needed for this arrangement. It is built up on florist's foam taped to a saucer, and the flowers and foliage cover both almost completely.

Flowers and foliage

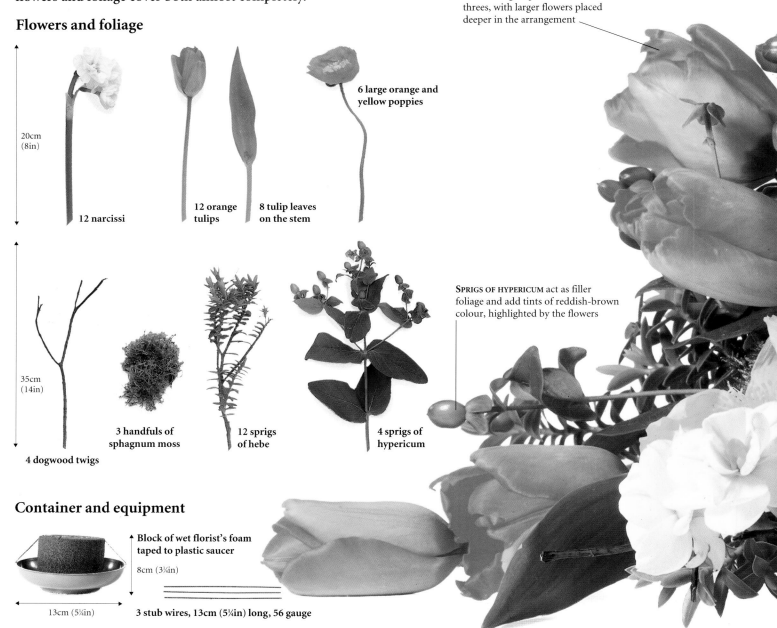

20cm (8in)

12 narcissi

12 orange tulips

8 tulip leaves on the stem

6 large orange and yellow poppies

TULIPS are grouped in twos and threes, with larger flowers placed deeper in the arrangement

35cm (14in)

4 dogwood twigs

3 handfuls of sphagnum moss

12 sprigs of hebe

4 sprigs of hypericum

SPRIGS OF HYPERICUM act as filler foliage and add tints of reddish-brown colour, highlighted by the flowers

Container and equipment

Block of wet florist's foam taped to plastic saucer

8cm (3¼in)

13cm (5¼in)

3 stub wires, 13cm (5¼in) long, 56 gauge

DOGWOOD TWIGS break
out of the outline and
enhance the natural look

DELICATE NARCISSI visually lift the
arrangement, the yellow centres
highlighting the poppies and tulips

THE FINISHED EFFECT
*While the symmetry of the display gives
a slightly formal quality, the overall
effect is cheerful, casual and rustic.*

TWIGS introduce a
rustic element and
emphasize the red
hues in the flowers

MAKING THE TABLE CENTRE

First prepare the flowers and foliage (see page 174).
Set the height and width of the arrangement
with the dogwood twigs. The rest of the
flowers and foliage are grouped by type
around these points.

POSITION THREE TWIGS
equally around the sides,
with one in the centre, and
place moss between them

SLOPE THE OUTSIDE TWIGS down
from the florist's foam by pushing
the stems in at an upward angle

GROUP SPRIGS OF HEBE in
threes around each twig

*1 Space three dogwood twigs around the sides
of the foam, each a third of the way round
and angled down, and place one in the top.
Attach the moss between the twigs with stub
wires bent into hairpin hooks (see page 177).*

*2 Push sprigs of hebe in groups of three into
the foam next to each twig. The sprigs in
each group should be of different lengths.
Angle them down at the sides, and push fuller
sprigs further into the arrangement.*

*3 Divide the narcissi into groups of three,
making sure they are of varying lengths.
Push in each group next to a twig, on the
opposite side from the hebe. Angle the heads to
face in different directions.*

ADD NARCISSI in groups of
three around the twigs

KEEP FULLER NARCISSI STEMS
short, and push deeper into
the arrangement

POINT FLOWER HEADS in
different directions

4 Add tulips in groups of two or three. Push them in at different lengths, keeping larger blooms deeper in the arrangement. Push in cut-off stems with leaves still attached next to the flowers.

TULIPS are added to the sides and top in groups

PUSH IN SEPARATE TULIP STEMS with leaves next to the flowers

LUSCIOUS LARGE POPPY HEADS act as recessionary flowers

5 Place the large orange and yellow poppies deep and more centrally within the arrangement to fill it out. Finally, push in sprigs of hypericum at different lengths among the groups of flowers.

LONGER TULIP STEMS slope down from the sides

Alternative Colourway

Substitute hyacinths, anemones and ivy for the tulips, poppies and hypericum to create a completely different yet equally bold colour combination. You may like to combine the bright orange and deep purple colours for a really stunning result.

Alternative flowers and foliage

12 sprigs of variegated ivy

9 purple hyacinths

12 purple anemones

HYACINTH HEADS replace the tulips

BLUE THEME
For a less spring-like, yet just as dramatic effect, replace the orange flowers with deep purple anemones and hyacinths. Place larger, more open flowers toward the centre of the display.

VARIEGATED IVY is substituted for the reddish hypericum

BASKET ARRANGEMENT

THE BASKET ARRANGEMENT has become a popular request for florists. Baskets themselves appear in many guises, and fashion trends ensure that their shapes and the materials used to make them constantly change. Here, I have used a very traditional basket, round in shape with a good depth to fill with florist's foam.

40cm (16in)

45cm (18in)

DESIGN TIP
The flowers and foliage have been positioned to follow the form of the basket. They mirror the rounded shape, creating the impression of a sphere.

MATERIALS AND EQUIPMENT
To prevent water leaking out, a plastic bowl is placed in the basket with the wet florist's foam secured inside with tape.

Flowers and foliage

55cm
(21½in)

6 mauve mop-headed hydrangeas   **20 pink roses**   **3 stems of spray roses**   **10 heads of dill**

THE FINISHED EFFECT
Country garden-style mop-headed hydrangeas and dill complement the rustic basket, while classic pink roses introduce a formal element. These qualities combine to create a traditional basket arrangement, appropriate for many occasions.

FOUR VARIETIES OF FOLIAGE ——
set the width and height of the arrangement

BEAUTIFULLY TINTED ——
hydrangeas add fullness and body to the finished piece

45cm
(18in)

10 sprigs of skimmia   **10 sprigs of prunus**   **10 sprigs of senecio**   **10 sprigs of stephanandra**

Basket and equipment

▶ **Block of wet florist's foam taped to plastic bowl**

9cm
(3½in)

20cm (8in)

Round traditional basket

13cm
(5¼in)

32cm (12⅝in)

SPRAY ROSES have attractive buds and fill in spaces around the larger roses

RED-BROWN PRUNUS highlights the red shades in the hydrangeas

HEADS OF DILL are kept level with the larger pink roses

DESPITE THEIR SUBTLE colour, roses remain the dominant focal flower

MAKING THE BASKET

The height and width of the display are established by four types of foliage, each one filling a quarter of the base. The flowers are then added, one variety at a time, starting with the larger blooms.

KEEP LONGER SHOOTS in the centre of the display

1 Place the plastic bowl with the wet florist's foam in the basket. Cut the skimmia to varying lengths and push into the foam to fill in a quarter of the surface. Repeat with the prunus.

WET FLORIST'S FOAM is taped to the plastic bowl

DARKER-COLOURED PRUNUS is kept to the back of the display

2 Trim the senecio and stephanandra to varying lengths. Fill in the remaining two quarters of the foam with groups of each. Use longer lengths toward the centre and the sides to establish the outline of the arrangement.

EACH TYPE OF FOLIAGE fills a quarter of the surface area

Viewed from above

SET HYDRANGEA HEADS deep into the foliage

WEAVE ROSES down from the top to the sides of the arrangement

KEEP SPRAY ROSES at a higher level than the roses

3 Trim the hydrangea stems down to about 15cm (6in) and push them into the foam among the foliage. Group them toward the sides and centre of the basket, keeping them deep within the foliage.

4 Trim the roses to 20cm (8in) and group them between the hydrangeas. Trim the lower leaves from the spray roses. Push into the top of the display, next to and slightly higher than the larger roses. Finally, add the dill.

Alternative Colourway

Blazing orange roses, reddish mop-headed hydrangeas and burnished butterfly weed change the quite formal appearance of the basket to an exuberant, glowing, autumnal arrangement.

Alternative flowers

6 reddish mop-headed hydrangeas

25 large orange roses

10 sprigs of butterfly weed

RICHLY TINTED BUTTERFLY WEED breaks up the larger shapes

LUSCIOUS ROSES glow strongly as the main focal flower

FIERY ORANGE TONES
Hydrangeas in shades of green and red replace the mauve variety; large-headed, open roses in vibrant orange tones replace the pink roses; and butterfly weed takes the place of the lime and white dill. The foliage remains the same.

Rose Basket

Echoing the flat, rounded shape of the basket arrangement on pages 44–47, this display is based on a wintery white and green theme. Random brushstrokes of white acrylic paint on the basket create a fresh, frosted effect. The flowers and foliage will last for about ten days if the florist's foam is kept moist, and wilted blooms and leaves can easily be replaced, if necessary.

LICHEN MOSS, attached with hairpin hooks, conceals the florist's foam

WHITE ROSE HEADS are simply pushed into wet florist's foam

ORNAMENTAL CABBAGE LEAVES are pushed down into the foam

ROSE LEAVES provide dark foliage to enhance the cabbage leaves and white roses

THE BASKET is lined with plastic and filled with blocks of wet florist's foam

EXTRAVAGANT VASE DISPLAY
I have clustered together an abundance of flowers by type almost to overpower a simple, dark green, glossy container.

VASE DISPLAYS

TO MY MIND there is nothing more simple or spontaneous than arranging fresh flowers in a vase. One of the most commonly attempted forms of flower arrangement, vase displays lend instant freshness and colour to any setting.

A vase and its flowers should always work together, interacting to create a unified composition; whatever its style, a display must also sit comfortably in its surroundings. Even buying carefully colour-coordinated bunches of flowers, ready-arranged to drop into a vase, does not guarantee a successful display if you fail to consider the style and final position of the container.

Flowers totally alter the look of a vessel, whether a glass vase or a wooden bowl, so choose varieties that balance well. Tall flowers with individual florets growing low on the stem, such as gladioli, are a natural choice for upright, tall containers, but don't be afraid to trim taller flowers, too. Lofty and majestic hippeastrum, for example, when cut down take on a fuller, more luxurious appearance. Simplicity is vital for modern displays, and narrow-necked vases that keep a minimal number of stems close together and upright ensure the perfect look of cool sophistication. Provençal bowls and jugs, with their rustic associations, call for an abundance of colour and texture, while flared vases need an ample amount of foliage to prevent the flowers from falling to the edge. Clear glass vases, with their relative anonymity, suit almost any setting and also allow you to make a feature of the stems.

Vase displays can last for a long time if you care for them well. Prepare the stems before starting to arrange (see pages 174–175) to keep them healthy and strong. Make sure the water is clean by replacing it every two days: stand the arrangement under running water until all the old water has been flushed out. Add flower food to the water whenever possible.

Flared Vase Display
Page 52

Cylindrical Vases
Page 54

Low Bowl Display
Page 56

Formal Country Display
Page 62

FLARED VASE DISPLAY

THE DIAMETER OF A VASE'S MOUTH will help determine the type and quantity of flowers to be used in it. This elegant flared vase calls for tall, strong, supple flowers, such as tulips, that will lend themselves to its shape while supporting one another as the stems intertwine.

MAKING THE ARRANGEMENT

Choose tulip and eucalyptus stems about twice the height of the container. Prepare all the flower and foliage stems before arranging (see page 174).

MATERIALS AND EQUIPMENT

Flowers and foliage

45cm (18in)

30 pink tulips   **15 lengths of eucalyptus**

Container

Flared glass vase

25cm (10in)

25cm (10in)

TULIP STEMS FOLLOW the line of the vase

LEAVE ONE OR TWO LEAVES on the tulip stems

ADD LENGTHS OF EUCALYPTUS between the tulips

STEMS have been scraped down and trimmed off neatly

1 Fill the vase three quarters' full with water. Insert between seven and ten tulips, spiralling them around the edge of the vase to follow its angle and lean over the edge.

STEMS below the water-line have been stripped of leaves

2 Add lengths of eucalyptus between the tulip stems, making sure they lean over the vase at the same angle as the flowers.

Flared Vase Display

PINK TULIPS are complemented by hints of mauve in the eucalyptus

DELICATE SMALL-LEAVED EUCALYPTUS sprigs contrast with the large, smooth tulip blooms and leaves

3 Fill in the display with the remaining tulips and eucalyptus. Keep the taller stems toward the centre and angle the leaves to follow the line of the flower heads.

THICK, GREEN TULIP STEMS fill out the vase and provide light colour for contrast

50cm (20in)

55cm (22in)

DESIGN TIP
The overall display is about twice the height of the vase, and the flowers and foliage form a dome shape above the container. The display is slightly wider than it is high.

CYLINDRICAL VASES

THE DIFFERING DIMENSIONS AND COLOURS of these two cylindrical vases call for displays quite specific to each. Low, wide containers require a compact display of short, grouped flowers, while taller, narrower vases can support longer, more elegant stems and foliage on different levels. Choose flowers to highlight the texture of the container, too.

MATERIALS AND EQUIPMENT – Low Bowl

Flowers

Container

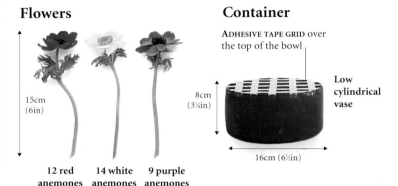

15cm (6in)

ADHESIVE TAPE GRID over the top of the bowl

8cm (3¼in)

Low cylindrical vase

16cm (6½in)

12 red anemones   **14 white anemones**   **9 purple anemones**

MATERIALS AND EQUIPMENT – Tall Vase

Flowers and foliage   **Container**

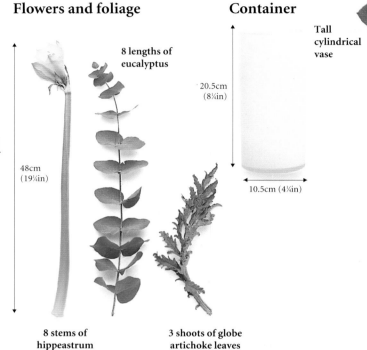

8 lengths of eucalyptus

Tall cylindrical vase

20.5cm (8¼in)

10.5cm (4¼in)

48cm (19¼in)

8 stems of hippeastrum   **3 shoots of globe artichoke leaves**

LOW, VIBRANT DISPLAY
The dramatic blue colour and low, wide dimensions of this bowl govern the style of display to be created in it. Bold-coloured, flat, round anemones are cut short and massed together in a low arrangement, grouped by colour in random batches. The bowl is as important a feature as the flowers, and the display is equally effective viewed side-on or from above.

RED AND PURPLE ANEMONES are grouped toward the edge of the bowl

THE FLOWERS, cut to a length of 7cm (2¾in), are inserted through the adhesive tape grid

THE SHAPE AND COLOUR of the container are complemented by the velvety, intense-coloured anemones

Viewed from above

LONGER STEMS of hippeastrum are positioned toward the back of the display

STEMS OF EUCALYPTUS fill out the display, lending height and width

GLOBE ARTICHOKE LEAVES inserted at the base of the arrangement balance the display and hang down to conceal the top of the vase

TALL, FRONT-FACING DISPLAY

Serrated silvery globe artichoke leaves juxtapose with the smooth green eucalyptus, while white hippeastrum flowers dominate the display with their colour and shape. The height of the vase allows flowers and foliage to extend out quite far from the sides, but the display would look equally impressive if more contained and column-like.

FROSTED GLASS partly obscures the stems and exaggerates the silvery tones of the flowers and foliage

Side view

LOW BOWL DISPLAY

WHILE LARGE FLOWERS are usually more fitting for tall containers, they can look just as stunning in a low bowl. Here, I have cut hippeastrum stems right down for a display, best seen from above, that allows the viewer to appreciate the luxurious openness of the large, fleshy blooms.

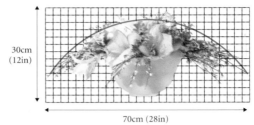

30cm (12in)

70cm (28in)

DESIGN TIP
The ingredients have been arranged low in the bowl, making the display as high as the container and twice as wide.

MATERIALS AND EQUIPMENT

Flowers and foliage

20cm (8in)

20 sprigs of broom

5 stems of peach hippeastrum

5 stems of white hippeastrum

8 sprigs of cineraria

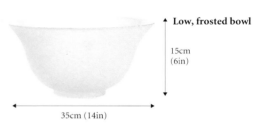

Container

Low, frosted bowl

15cm (6in)

35cm (14in)

MAKING THE ARRANGEMENT

No tape grid is necessary for this display: flowers and foliage are kept compact, supporting each other.

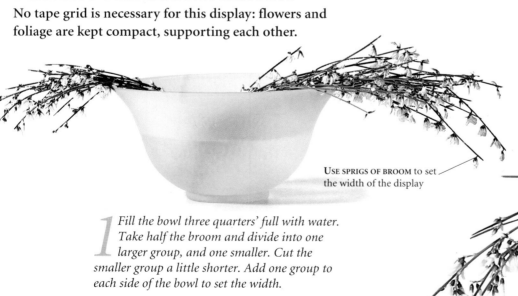

USE SPRIGS OF BROOM to set the width of the display

1 Fill the bowl three quarters' full with water. Take half the broom and divide into one larger group, and one smaller. Cut the smaller group a little shorter. Add one group to each side of the bowl to set the width.

2 Fill the centre of the bowl with hippeastrum, keeping the colours separate. Place the larger flowers most centrally, with narrower heads and buds leaning over the edge of the bowl.

KEEP LARGER BLOOMS central and low

LET SMALLER FLOWERS lean over the edges of the bowl

GROUP PEACH HIPPEASTRUM together

Viewed from a higher angle

USE DELICATE CINERARIA to fill out the arrangement and contrast with the heavy hippeastrum blooms

FROSTED GLASS CONCEALS the stems and blends with the pale flowers and foliage

3 Add sprigs of cineraria. Use them to fill out the display and hang over the bowl, subtly linking the hippeastrum and broom. Add more sprigs of broom around the front and back of the bowl.

Low Rustic Bowl

A beautiful, wide, low, Provençal bowl has been filled with a lavish selection of fresh, summery flowers that spill out and tumble over the sides. The flamboyance and abundance of the display are a result of its width and height: it is over three times the height of the bowl and twice as wide. The flowers have been arranged in the same way as those on pages 56–57, building up from the sides, but the extra width of the bowl accommodates a much taller and wider display.

SPIKY SEA HOLLY is a foil to the other soft, less rigid flowers, and echoes the blue of the bowl

LIGHT PINK FEATHERY ASTILBE contrast with the dark red snapdragons

STRONG, BUT SUPPLE SNAPDRAGONS splay over the edge of the bowl, establishing the width

TRAILING TENDRILS OF JASMINE enhance the spontaneous effect and add a sweet, heady scent to the display

THE DUSKY BLUE EARTHENWARE BOWL provides a dark base for the profusion of colours in the display

VIBRANT DELPHINIUMS grouped together form the highest points of the display

SPRIGS OF SCENTED LILAC fill out one side

TINY YELLOW SPRAY ROSES are bunched around a group of larger pink roses

TRAILING FOLIAGE makes the display appear wider and balances the high delphiniums

A SINGLE LARGE HYDRANGEA LEAF, placed asymmetrically, provides structure and sets off the less substantial ivy and jasmine

59

SIMPLE MODERN VESSEL

DISPLAYS MADE IN WIDE CONTAINERS, such as this loosely arranged modern winter display, may need some extra support. I find it useful to use chicken wire, folded and curved to fill out the container, so that flower and foliage stems can be pushed in through the gaps.

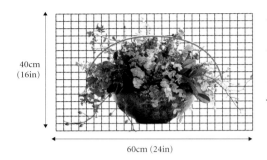

40cm (16in)

60cm (24in)

DESIGN TIP
The display mirrors the shape of the bowl, with longer lengths of foliage extending upward and from the sides to break the outline.

MATERIALS AND EQUIPMENT

Flowers and foliage

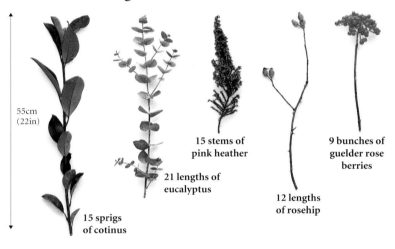

55cm (22in)

15 sprigs of cotinus

21 lengths of eucalyptus

15 stems of pink heather

12 lengths of rosehip

9 bunches of guelder rose berries

Container and equipment

Plastic bowl filled with chicken wire secured with stub wires and florist's tape

12cm (4¾in)

20cm (8in)

Wooden bowl

16cm (6½in)

40cm (16in)

MAKING THE DISPLAY

Fill the plastic bowl with chicken wire, twist stub wires around the chicken wire on each side, and tape them to the outside of the bowl with florist's tape.

PUSH IN random groups of three eucalyptus lengths

1 Fill the plastic bowl three quarters' full with water and place in the wooden container. Trim the cotinus and eucalyptus to 30cm (12in) and insert into the chicken wire. Add the eucalyptus in groups of three between the cotinus.

ANGLE the stems so they point out slightly

2 *Cut the stems of heather to 20cm (8in) long. Push them into the centre of the chicken wire among the cotinus and eucalyptus to form a domed shape in the centre of the arrangement.*

PLACE HEATHER stems in the centre of the foliage

3 *Cut the rosehips to 50cm (20in) long, and push into the plastic bowl to trail over the sides of the wooden container. Finally, push the bunches of berries deeper in the display.*

LET LENGTHS of rosehip extend furthest from the wooden bowl

PUSH IN BUNCHES of berries to fill out the display

Formal Country Display

An unusual, elegant container introduces a stylized element to a casual arrangement for a modern setting. Using chicken wire for support, as on pages 60–61, I have arranged large rounded blooms and trailing ivy low and wide in a galvanized metal container resting on a wrought iron and wicker stand. The curved feet of the stand, sculptural lilies and long lengths of ivy create a decorative art nouveau effect.

DELICATE HELENIUM lightens the mood with its bright colour and rustic charm

Formal Country Display

ORANGE ROSES blend with the deep purples and pinks of the other flowers

THE ELEGANT LINES of the lilies promote a flowing, sinuous feel

MOP-HEADED HYDRANGEAS help shape the display with their luxurious, rounded surfaces

TRAILING IVY lends a sweeping line to the display, echoing the curves of the stand

TRAINED CHRISTMAS RING
Two ivy plants have been trained to climb around a frame and form a ring, echoing the traditional symbol of the Christmas wreath. A bow made from crimson wired French ribbon adds a festive touch and matches the colouring of the pot.

PLANTED ARRANGEMENTS

A PLANTED BOWL immediately fills me with a sense of panic. I hate with a vengeance those pudding basins with a mix of tropical looking plants and a token African violet. They represent everything that is outdated. At last there is a new look for planted displays. Gone is the plastic bowl, in come the basket, wooden trug and Provençal pottery. Out goes the tropical house plant mix, and in comes the solid, one-plant variety in striking colours, potted *en masse*.

For inspiration, study the groupings of plants in gardens or hedgerows. A large range of plants can be transported from the flower-bed to planted containers – and from the vegetable patch and herb garden, too. If mixing species together in one display, choose plants of similar longevity and flowering times, with compatible watering, heat and light requirements.

When you choose a vessel, make sure it complements the plant not only in colour but also in style. Baskets or rustic pottery are ideal counterparts to cineraria or tiny spring narcissi, which lend themselves to a country or Provençal look. Stone or metal urns overflowing with hydrangeas or orchids have a grander, more decadent aura. And even the most unassuming, drab pot can be transformed by the vibrant colour and bold shape of a hyacinth with its sweet, heady scent that lingers for days. Topiary plants, trained, grown and trimmed to shape, then planted in terracotta pots not only create a sense of drama in the sweeping grounds of stately homes, but on a smaller scale bring character to patios, doorsteps and window sills of more modest homes.

Even the most understated flower or plant can be made to look really special when planted in a suitable container, and because these displays are so long-lasting, they make attractive gifts. Planted arrangements are also low on maintenance and require little practical expertise: the only skill you need to learn is how to line porous containers that have no saucer with plastic to prevent leakage. It is important, too, to choose a good potting compost.

Planted Trug
Page 66

Summer Herb Arrangement
Page 72

Potted Plant Display
Page 74

PLANTED TRUG

A VARIATION ON THE MORE TRADITIONAL planted basket, this arrangement in a trug is easily assembled and makes an ideal gift. I have chosen hardy heather, crimson spray roses and deep red pansies to complement the country trug and form a welcoming winter display. A cheerful bow made of red ribbon makes the trug particularly appropriate for the weeks before Christmas.

MATERIALS AND EQUIPMENT
Line the trug with plastic sheeting before planting the potted flowers to prevent water leaking out.

Plants and decoration

32cm (12¾in)

4 pink heather plants

3 crimson spray rose plants

15cm (6in)

3 red pansy plants

5 handfuls of bun moss

50cm (20in) wired French ribbon, 2.5cm (1in) wide

Container and equipment

↑ **Painted trug**

35cm (14in)

33cm (13¼in)

Plastic sheeting, 50 x 50cm (20 x 20in)

Broken terracotta pieces (crocks)

2.5kg (5lb) bag of potting soil

A ROW OF PINK HEATHER sets
the height of the display

THE FINISHED EFFECT
*Pink heather and deep crimson spray roses
are set off by a small group of pansies in one
corner of the trug. A red bow maintains the
opulent, rich image and introduces a vibrant,
festive feeling to the country arrangement.*

PANSIES are grouped
together in one corner

A GLEAMING
CRIMSON BOW
enhances the
festive element

Viewed from a higher angle

PLANTING THE TRUG

Place half the soil in the lined trug before
removing the plants from their pots. Once they
are all correctly positioned in the trug, add the
rest of the soil and the bun moss.

POSITION HEATHER PLANTS SO
that the flowers extend
beyond the handle

LINE THE TRUG with plastic
sheeting to protect it from
moisture in the soil

*1 Line the trug with the square of plastic
sheeting so that it hangs over the sides.
Strew the terracotta crocks evenly over
the base and then add half the potting soil
and firm it down.*

*2 Carefully remove the heather plants
from their pots and place them in a line
across the back of the trug, so that they
stand taller than the handle. Angle the plants
on the outer edges slightly over the rim.*

PLACE SPRAY ROSES in
front of the heather

*3 Remove the spray roses from their pots
and place in front of the heather plants.
Position them in a line, starting at the
left side of the trug, and leave some space in
the right-hand corner.*

GROUP PANSIES in the right-hand corner

ADD BUN MOSS to conceal the soil

4 Remove the pansies from their pot, and group them in the front right-hand corner of the trug, next to the spray roses. Add the rest of the soil around the plants, up to 2.5cm (1in) below the rim of the trug.

5 Trim off the plastic sheeting to just below the inner rim of the trug, slightly above soil level, and add bun moss around the base of the plants. Finally, tie a bow around the handle with the wired ribbon.

Alternative Colourway

Change the single colour theme to a mixed theme, using the same type of flowers, but in different colours. Keep the same ribbon to link in with the heathers retained in the back of the trug.

Alternative flowers

3 white spray rose plants

3 purple and white pansy plants

WHITE SPRAY ROSES replace the crimson variety

FRESH WINTER TRUG
Introducing white spray roses and purple and white pansies breaks up the uniformity of the display and lightens the emphasis. The overall display is brighter and fresher.

Planted Spring Bulbs

Narcissi, scilli and other bulbs potted in interesting containers, such as these rough-hewn wooden trugs, form delightful, long-lasting decorations that bring the first scents of spring indoors. Choose flowers with unopened buds and line the trugs with plastic before potting. The arrangements will last for two to three weeks if kept moist and cool, and they make charming gifts for Easter or Mothering Sunday.

THE DIFFERING LENGTHS of flower stems on each bulb break up the uniformity

TALLER SCILLI are planted near the centre

SMALL PEBBLES AND LICHEN moss conceal the earth and bulbs

THE GREEN-STAINED TRUG provides colour contrast with the light lichen moss and complements the delicate scilli

NARCISSI are planted irregularly with roughly the same amount of earth surrounding each bulb

THIN TWIGS are used to form a decorative fence around the arrangement

THE RAFFIA used to bind the twig fence adds to the rustic look

BUN MOSS is pressed between the bulbs to conceal the earth

THE SIMPLE UNPAINTED TRUG complements the twigs and yellow narcissi

SUMMER HERB ARRANGEMENT

THE DECORATIVE USE OF HERBS need not be limited to the herb garden outdoors. Here, I have potted different herbs in old terracotta pots, disguising the soil with moss, and grouped them together to form a kitchen window display. Similar herbs planted in an unusual low container form a long-lasting, aromatic composition.

SINGLE POTTED HERBS
When potting herbs individually, choose varieties that look quite different (allowing for culinary needs if you must). Grouped together, they form an eye-catching arrangement.

THE CURRY PLANT, with its delicate, silvery fronds, introduces a cool, pale colour

TALL, NARROW STEMS of hyssop contrast with the single, fuller sage plant

BROAD-LEAVED PURPLE SAGE is a familiar culinary herb suited to a simple kitchen arrangement

Summer Herb Arrangement

STRAIGHT, SUPPLE OREGANO plants provide height at the back of the display

TALL HYSSOP SHOOTS add colour to the top of the display

INDOOR HERB GARDEN
Herbs have been chosen for their contrasting shapes, textures and colours to create a large potted arrangement. Taller plants are kept toward the back of the display, while shorter, bushy herbs fill out the centre and front.

PURPLE-LEAVED SAGE is used as the middle-level herb in the centre of the arrangement

ROSEMARY trails over the front, adding movement and balance

POTTED PLANT DISPLAY

SIMPLE PLANTED ARRANGEMENTS of one type of plant make appealing decorations that are very easy to maintain. Here, I have grouped two colour co-ordinated potted containers to form a homely composition that really displays the bold colours of the flowers well.

MATERIALS AND EQUIPMENT

Choose plants that complement the colour and shape of the containers. Make sure they are of similar height, at the same stage of development and have flowers with a long life-span.

Plants and moss

35cm (14in)

1 large primula plant

5 small primula plants

10 handfuls of carpet moss

Containers and equipment

15cm (6in)

35cm (14in)

15cm (6in)

1 large, wide container and 1 cylindrical pot with a saucer

Plastic sheeting, 50 x 50cm (20 x 20in)

Broken terracotta pieces (crocks)

2.5kg (5lb) bag of potting soil

A SINGLE TALL PRIMULA complements the small cylindrical pot

THE MAUVE CONTAINER clashes delightfully with the deep red primula

POTTING THE PLANTS
Line the container without a saucer with plastic sheeting, so that it hangs 5cm (2in) over the edge. Scatter crocks over the base of both containers, and add some soil. Remove the plants from their pots and place in the containers, filling soil around them up to 2.5cm (1in) from the top of the pot. Firm the soil, water well, and trim the plastic sheeting to just above the soil level. Add moss to conceal the soil.

PRIMULA HEADS echo the colour of the container

FIRST LINE THE LARGE CONTAINER with plastic sheeting to prevent water seeping out

SOME PLANTS lean slightly toward the edge

CARPET MOSS conceals the soil and accentuates the unaffected charm

THE FINISHED EFFECT
Intense clashing red and purple primulas have been chosen to correspond with the colours of the containers, and the light green ribbing on the smaller pot is picked up by the veins in the leaves.

CASCADING URN
*Flamboyant foliage and vibrant flowers
cascade over a classical urn, creating an
opulent, dramatic spectacle.*

LARGE-SCALE ARRANGEMENTS

FEW OF US ARE FORTUNATE ENOUGH to have inherited the family stately home, with a vast hallway that requires a huge fresh flower arrangement every week of the year. For most people a large arrangement is only called for on special occasions – Christmas, Thanksgiving, religious celebrations, harvest, weddings, christenings or perhaps a party, birthday, anniversary or business conference. These occasions demand large, eye-catching displays of flowers and bold statements and extravagant effects are the order of the day.

Mantelpiece Arrangement
Page 78

I believe that a large-scale arrangement needs a little more attention to theme than a smaller, everyday display. Simply increasing the quantity of smaller flowers often leads to an undefined mass of colour that fails to engage or excite the viewer. The choice of vessel can alter this immediately. An urn or pedestal creates instant drama and classical grace. A mantelpiece structure allows foliage and flowers to tumble and curl around its framework. Swags or garlands require no extra trimmings. Hung in a prominent position, they enliven even the most sombre of spaces.

Making full use of accessories in a large display helps dictate the tenor of an occasion. Voluptuous twists and drapes of deep red velvet bring warmth to winter or Christmas arrangements. Fruit and vegetables used in an innovative way reflect the season and can also add a touch of humour to a display, while enhancing the shape and texture of the flowers.

Pedestal Display
Page 82

When planning a large-scale arrangement do make sure there is ample space for it. Forcing a display into a tight area immediately dampens its impact and creates a crowded atmosphere. Choose larger flowers where possible and group them together to form bold blocks of colour. If roses or even smaller flowers are required, it is easy for them to become lost, so mass them together to ensure that they can be noticed from far away.

Long Table Decoration
Page 86

MANTELPIECE ARRANGEMENT

THE SOBER ELEGANCE and straight lines of a mantelpiece often demand a formal flower display, but here, to create a freer, more spontaneous effect, I have combined informal potted plants, foliage and moss in a relaxed, abundant arrangement that covers the entire mantelpiece. The dark mauve ornamental cabbages, heather and pansies lend depth to the display.

DEEP PINK HEATHER softens the arrangement and lends height

THE FINISHED EFFECT
A rich combination of textures and surprising lack of symmetry in the arrangement produce a naturally impromptu display.

OPEN, ROUNDED ornamental cabbages are instantly eye-catching

RED PANSIES provide tiny pools of colour

TRAILING IVY counterbalances the height of the arrangement and adds fluid lines

MATERIALS AND EQUIPMENT

A layer of plastic sheeting protects the mantelpiece
and is concealed with clumps of moss and trailing ivy.

Equipment

Plastic sheeting,
20cm x 1.2m (8in x 4ft)

12 stub wires,
26cm (10½in) long, 71 gauge

Plants and moss

30cm
(12in)

**3 variegated
ivy plants**

**2 purple
ornamental cabbages**

**2 pink
heather plants**

**5 red
pansy plants**

**12 handfuls of
bun moss**

**12 handfuls of
sphagnum moss**

CLUMPS OF MOSS conceal the
plastic sheeting and plant pots

MAKING THE ARRANGEMENT

Potted plants are placed at different angles and arranged asymmetrically along the mantelpiece. Clumps of moss conceal the pots and the gaps between them.

LAY DOWN plastic sheeting to protect the mantelpiece

KEEP the ornamental cabbage plants upright

PLACE TWO IVY PLANTS on their sides so that the shoots trail downward

1 Cover the mantelpiece with the black plastic sheeting. Place three ivy plants on top, two on their sides, as shown, and one upright.

2 Place two ornamental cabbages on the mantelpiece, next to the two pots of ivy lying on their sides.

3 Position two pots of heather on the mantelpiece, keeping them the same distance apart as the ornamental cabbages.

POSITION TALL HEATHER plants to offset the low, rounded cabbages

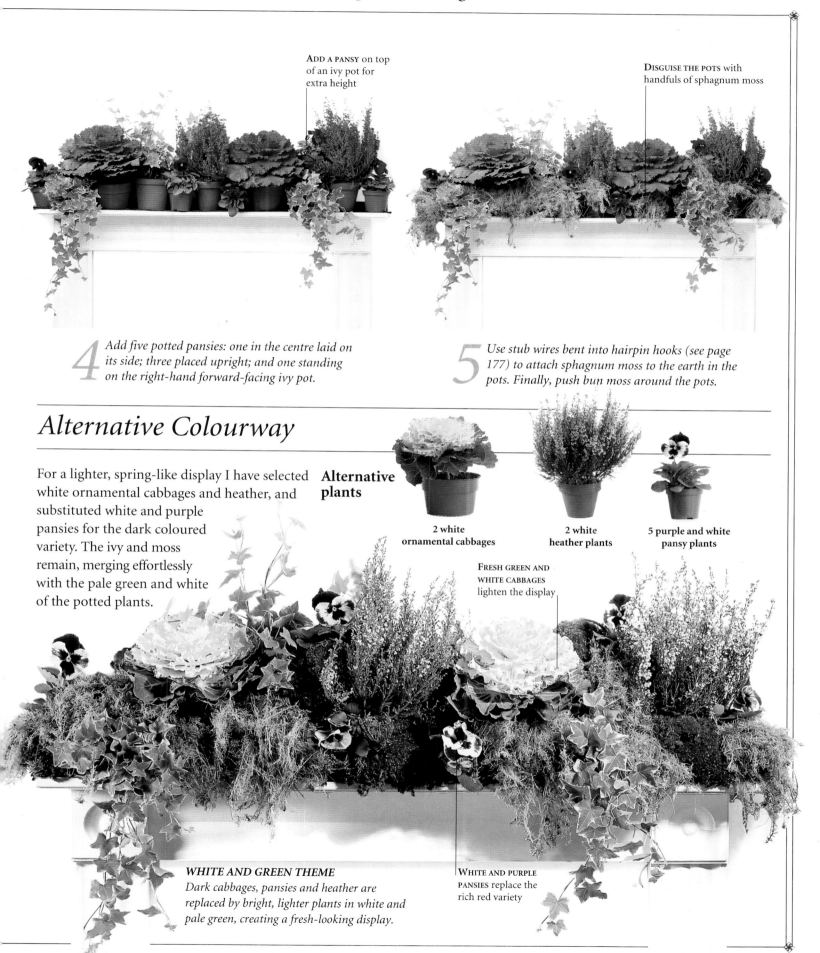

ADD A PANSY on top of an ivy pot for extra height

DISGUISE THE POTS with handfuls of sphagnum moss

4 *Add five potted pansies: one in the centre laid on its side; three placed upright; and one standing on the right-hand forward-facing ivy pot.*

5 *Use stub wires bent into hairpin hooks (see page 177) to attach sphagnum moss to the earth in the pots. Finally, push bun moss around the pots.*

Alternative Colourway

For a lighter, spring-like display I have selected white ornamental cabbages and heather, and substituted white and purple pansies for the dark coloured variety. The ivy and moss remain, merging effortlessly with the pale green and white of the potted plants.

Alternative plants

2 white ornamental cabbages

2 white heather plants

5 purple and white pansy plants

FRESH GREEN AND WHITE CABBAGES lighten the display

WHITE AND GREEN THEME
Dark cabbages, pansies and heather are replaced by bright, lighter plants in white and pale green, creating a fresh-looking display.

WHITE AND PURPLE PANSIES replace the rich red variety

PEDESTAL DISPLAY

AN OPULENT PEDESTAL DISPLAY brings splendour and high-drama to a large space, such as a hall or dining room. Make sure the pedestal stand and the arrangement merge comfortably: here I have used raffia to trail down the column, helping to integrate it with the main arrangement, but fabric or long lengths of foliage also work well.

MATERIALS AND EQUIPMENT

Flowers and foliage are built up on blocks of wet foam surrounded by chicken wire and taped to a wide, low bowl.

Flowers, foliage and decoration

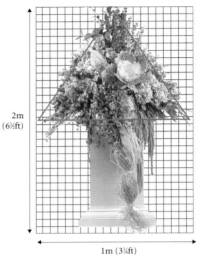

2m
(6½ft)

1m (3¼ft)

DESIGN TIP
The display is as high as the pedestal and twice as wide. The ingredients are placed asymmetrically and a large bunch of raffia trails down one side, forming a bond between the flowers and the column to balance the display visually.

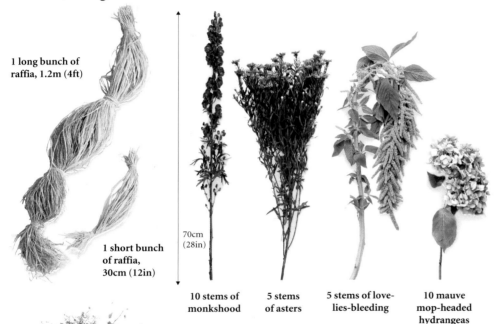

1 long bunch of
raffia, 1.2m (4ft)

1 short bunch
of raffia,
30cm (12in)

70cm
(28in)

10 stems of
monkshood

5 stems
of asters

5 stems of love-
lies-bleeding

10 mauve
mop-headed
hydrangeas

1 large variegated
ivy plant

1 ornamental
cabbage

75cm
(30in)

6 stems of
cotoneaster

15 lengths of
berried ivy

5 branches
of oak leaves

Equipment

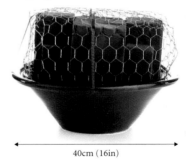

Blocks of wet florist's
foam wrapped in
chicken wire and
taped to a low bowl

20cm
(8in)

40cm (16in)

3 twigs,
15cm (6in) long

3 stub wires,
35cm (14in) long, 90 gauge

THE FINISHED EFFECT
Natural raffia and an ornamental cabbage immediately catch the eye and add an element of rustic simplicity to counteract the grand associations of the pedestal style.

A SMALL BUNCH of raffia continues the line of the longer trailing raffia tail

FLOWERS AND IVY break up the triangular outline created by the lengths of foliage

MOP-HEADED HYDRANGEAS are pushed deep into the display

DROOPING LOVE-LIES-BLEEDING gracefully leads the eye from the arrangement down the column

MAKING THE PEDESTAL DISPLAY

Both bunches of raffia are attached with stub wires twisted into double leg mounts (see page 177); all other ingredients are simply pushed into the wet florist's foam.

PUSH IN the foliage at slightly different lengths within each group

1 Place the bowl on the pedestal and attach the large bunch of raffia to the front right-hand corner of the foam. Cut the cabbage stem on a slant and push into the top right-hand corner. Push the twigs into the drainage holes in the ivy pot and press in by the cabbage.

HOOK ON the large raffia bunch with double leg mounts

2 Push the lengths of cotoneaster into the centre of the back of the foam to form the highest point of the display. Push the berried ivy into the upper left side, and the oak leaves into the lower right side.

FAN OUT the monkshood to fill in the triangular outline

3 Add the stems of monkshood to the right of the cotoneaster, slightly lower and fanning out down the side. Divide the asters into two groups. Push one group into the foam to the left of the ivy, angled downward, and add the other to the right of the cabbage.

SET THE WIDTH of the left side of the display with asters

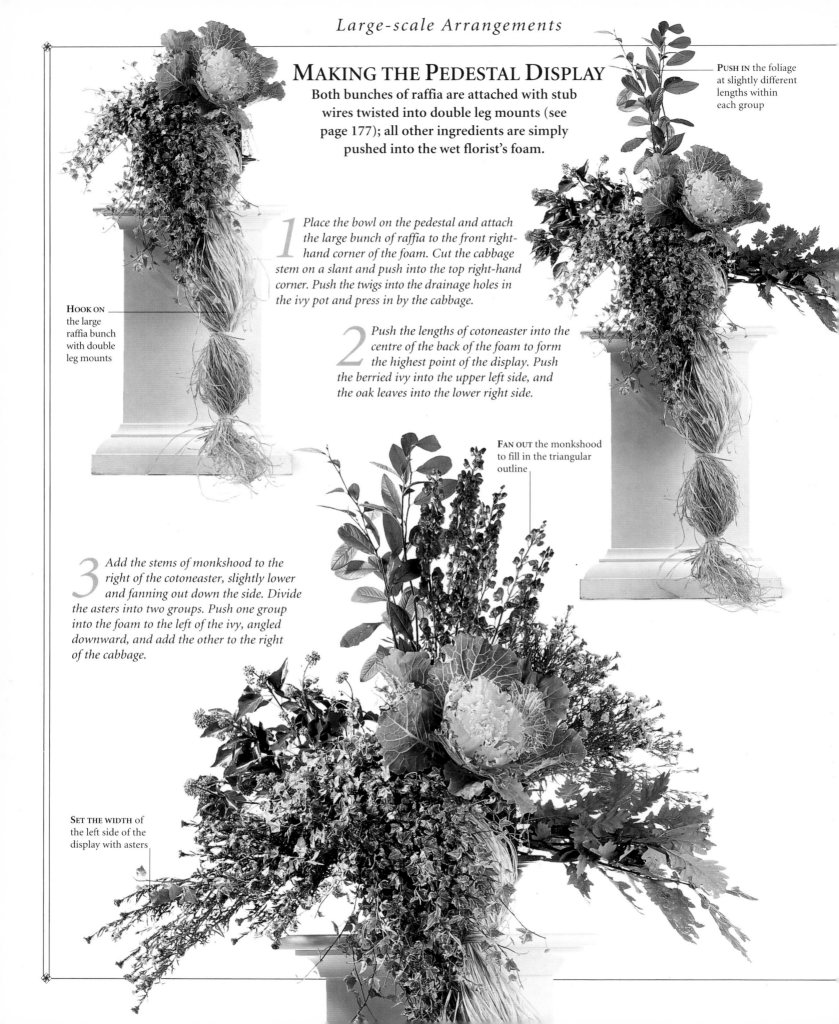

STEMS of love-lies-bleeding add a sense of asymmetry

PUSH IN STEMS of love-lies-bleeding to complement the raffia and conceal part of the pedestal

4 *Divide the love-lies-bleeding into two groups. Push one group into the foam to the right of the raffia, and add the other stems to the left of the ivy plant. Finally, push the hydrangeas deep into the arrangement and attach the shorter bunch of raffia with a double leg mount to the centre of the display, angled to continue the line of the longer length of raffia.*

Side view

LONG TABLE DECORATION

DESIGNED TO LIE ALONG THE CENTRE of a dining table, this fresh, informal centre-piece evokes a sense of eating alfresco indoors and can be made to fit any table. I have combined earthy moss and bark with delicate yellow flowers and foliage to create a decorative band that is reminiscent of a woodland floor or a spring flower bed. The tallest flowers on the top of the centre-piece are as long as the lengths of bark on the sides, creating a visually and structurally balanced band.

30cm (12in)

1.2m (4ft)

DESIGN TIP
The finished band can be bent to form a curved centre-piece for a table surface.

THE FINISHED EFFECT
Spring flowers and foliage are arranged in groups to look as if they are growing naturally out of the moss. Ivy is added between the other material, and appears to be growing from side to side along the band, reinforcing the natural look.

PLANTS ARE GROUPED by type, then placed at different heights and levels

ROSES AND ANGELICA are cut down short

PIECES OF BARK jut out from the arrangement

MATERIALS AND EQUIPMENT

You will need some plastic sheeting to cover the base of the band – this is to protect the table top from the moisture in the florist's foam.

Flowers and foliage

25cm (10in)

40 sprigs of broom (1 large branch)

25 narcissi

20 stems of achillea

10 stems of yellow spray roses

20 stems of mimosa

15cm (6in)

25 sprigs of ivy

10 sprigs of angelica

6 handfuls of carpet moss

15 pieces of bark, some moss-covered

Equipment

Chicken wire, 30 x 90cm (12 x 36in)

2 blocks of wet florist's foam

10 handfuls of sphagnum moss

30 stub wires, 35cm (14in) long, 90 gauge

Plastic sheeting, 15cm x 1m (6in x 3½ft)

IVY SPRIGS alternate from side to side, weaving along the band

MAKING THE DECORATION

The base is made by enclosing blocks of wet florist's foam in chicken wire. Handfuls of moss between the foam blocks act as hinges, making the band flexible.

CUT OFF THE CHICKEN WIRE 5cm (2in) from the ends of the foam

ATTACH PLASTIC SHEETING to protect the table surface from the wet florist's foam

CUT STUB WIRES in half and bend into hairpin hooks

1 Cut two blocks of soaked florist's foam into three sections each and place along the centre of the chicken wire, leaving a gap of 5cm (2in) between each block. Fill the gaps with handfuls of sphagnum moss.

2 Wrap the chicken wire around the foam and "sew" the sides together with stub wires. Fold the chicken wire round the end of the band like a parcel and push the ends back into the foam.

3 Place the plastic sheeting over the band, wrapping it 2.5cm (1in) over the sides. Attach it to the base by pushing stub wires bent into hairpin hooks (see page 177) through the plastic into the foam.

ADD SMALLER PIECES of bark in groups

ATTACH carpet moss with hairpin hooks

ANGLE THE BARK out toward the ends of the band, alternating from side to side

4 Turn the band over, as shown, and push pieces of bark into the sides and top of the florist's foam. Then hook on handfuls of carpet moss between them, using stub wires bent into hairpin hooks.

SET THE WIDTH AND HEIGHT of the band with sprigs of broom

WEND THE IVY from side to side as if growing over the bark

5 Push different-length sprigs of broom and ivy into the foam in groups between the bark.

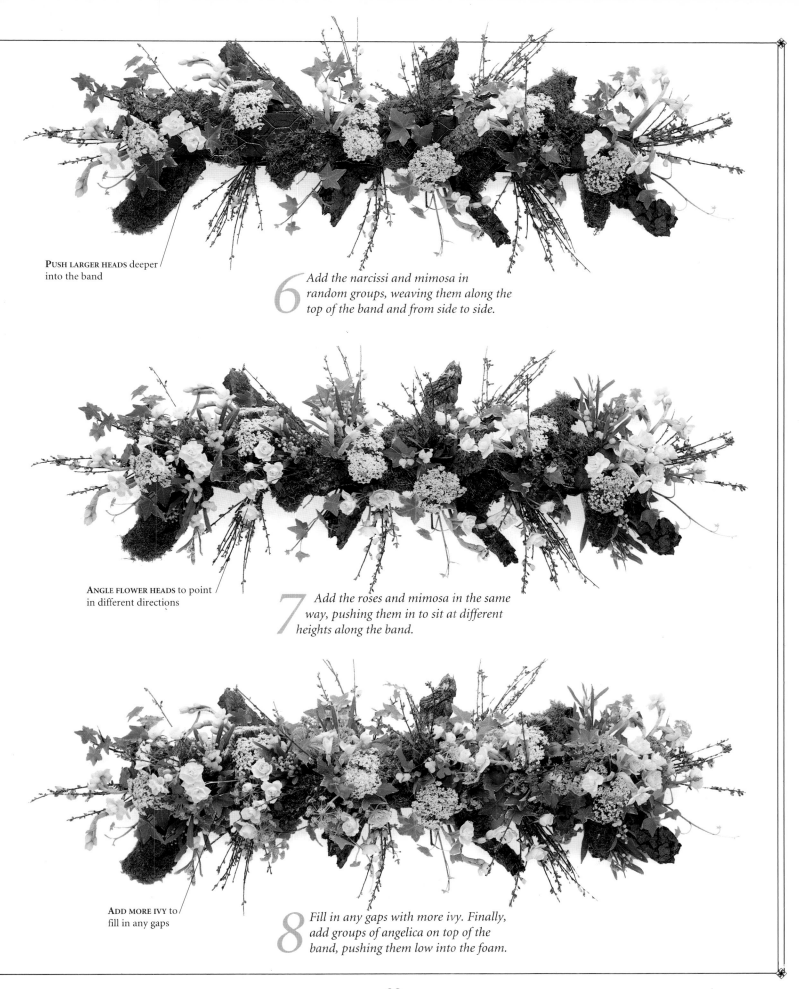

PUSH LARGER HEADS deeper into the band

6 *Add the narcissi and mimosa in random groups, weaving them along the top of the band and from side to side.*

ANGLE FLOWER HEADS to point in different directions

7 *Add the roses and mimosa in the same way, pushing them in to sit at different heights along the band.*

ADD MORE IVY to fill in any gaps

8 *Fill in any gaps with more ivy. Finally, add groups of angelica on top of the band, pushing them low into the foam.*

FRESH FLOWERS FOR SPECIAL OCCASIONS

No festivity is complete without the natural beauty of fresh flowers. Their uplifting colours and fragrances make them the essential finishing touch. When choosing flowers for special events, consider colour and form very carefully. Flamboyant blooms, such as sculptural lilies, immediately convey extravagance, while other flowers, such as romantic roses, have symbolic associations that may suit them to a particular occasion.

SIMPLE TIED POSY

THE TIED POSY, or hostess bouquet as it is sometimes known, has, I am pleased to say, gained in popularity over the traditional flat bouquet, and is a wonderful gift to give and receive. Flowers and foliage are spirally bound (see page 176) and the stems trimmed to one length, making the posy free-standing. It arrives ready to be placed in a vase, with no further arranging necessary by the recipient.

PALE GREEN EUCALYPTUS LEAVES break out from the dome shape, striking a note of informality

MAKING THE POSY
Spiral flowers and foliage and bind with string every three or four stems (see page 176) to create an even, dome shape and a neat waist that is later bound with ribbon. The binding point on each stem should be 20cm (8in) from the top of the flower, making a posy 40cm (16in) wide.

PURPLE LISIANTHUS has a delicacy that sets the tone of the display

SHINY RED ROSEHIP BERRIES add textural contrast and lift the muted green of the foliage

Viewed from above

THISTLE-LIKE CARDOONS introduce a rougher surface to vie with the delicate flowers

A SELECTION OF POSIES

WHEN MAKING SIMPLE TIED POSIES, make sure the effect is even and dome-shaped as you work, and that the stems are securely bound (see page 176) so that the finished posy is free standing. The distance between the top of the flower and the binding point should be the same for each stem, making the posy twice as wide as this length.

INFORMAL MODERN POSY
The influence of contemporary fashion and style trends extends to flower arranging, and this posy gains its young modern feel from the bold, bright, simple ingredients. Sunflowers, a favourite at the florist's, contrast with soft, supple timothy, variegated privet and strong, well-defined hosta leaves.

Viewed from above

VIBRANT SUNFLOWERS immediately catch the eye, giving the posy a sense of warmth and spontaneity

SUPPLE, FEATHERY TIMOTHY softens the effect of the hosta leaves and contrasts with the sunflowers

ALCHEMILLA provides a fresh, acid-lime colour and flowing line

COUNTRY POSY

For a casual, informal posy, I have combined several small-scale flowers and foliage in whites, purples and greens. No one colour predominates and there are few distinct shapes. The binding, made of plaited raffia, complements this bountiful, natural bouquet.

Viewed from above

HYPERICUM BERRIES contribute depth and deep colour

STEMS are spirally bound and tied with a raffia plait

SHINY RIBBON echoes the two-tone roses

CLASSIC FORMAL POSY

For a more formal special occasion, choose sophisticated flowers and rich binding ribbon, keeping ingredients simple, but select. Here, a classic rose dominates the traditional small posy, intermingled with mint and hypericum berries.

HINTS OF MAUVE in the mint complement the roses

BUTTONHOLES

WHILE BUTTONHOLES are particularly appropriate for special occasions such as weddings and seasonal celebrations, they can be worn to adorn everyday clothing, too. Choose blooms and foliage in prime condition, then wire and bind them together as near to the time of use as possible. Buttonholes will last for one day.

THREE SEA HOLLY LEAVES support a central head

MAKING BUTTONHOLES

Wire and bind the leaves and flowers individually (see pages 178–180), then bind them parallel to each other, one at a time, to avoid messy knots and twists of wire.

LARGER THREE-LEAFED SPRIG acts as the back support

1 Individually wire two single rose leaves and one three-leafed sprig with rose wires (see page 178). Bind the wire stems with gutta-percha tape (see page 180).

2 Wire the rose bud (see page 178) and bind the wire stems with tape, as before. Lay the rose against the three-leafed sprig and bind the two together with tape.

3 Bind the two single leaves one at a time to the front of the rose and the three-leafed sprig. Bend the wired leaves into shape and adjust the angle of the rose head if necessary.

SEA HOLLY
This simple buttonhole made from three sea holly leaves and one flower head makes an original, stylish decoration that can be worn with practically anything on any occasion.

FINE WIRE has been passed through the rose head and a heavier-gauge wire pushed up into the base

USE GUTTA-PERCHA TAPE to bind the wired stems together

SINGLE GARDENIA BLOOM supported by three dark green, glossy leaves

GARDENIA
For a classic buttonhole that makes a very special alternative to the usual carnation, try a single creamy gardenia against three leaves.

NATURAL STRING effectively conceals the gutta-percha tape, binding the flowers and leaves at one point

TULIPS
Two extravagant tulips and two leaves have been wired and bound together with gutta-percha tape. This is concealed by natural-coloured string. Casual and spontaneous, this type of artless buttonhole looks fresh and stylish.

TULIP FLOWER stems have been wired internally for support, so the wires do not show

FLOWERS AND LEAVES have been simply bound at one point, leaving bare stems exposed

LILY-OF-THE-VALLEY
Four stems of lily-of-the-valley have been wired and bound to three laurel leaves. Note that the stems have not been individually bound with gutta-percha tape – they are bound together at one point only.

LAUREL LEAF acts as the backdrop and support

ONE CINERARIA LEAF points downward, concealing the bound stems

A SINGLE IVY LEAF is attached to one side of the gerbera

MIXED FOLIAGE
Create a highly effective buttonhole without flowers by using a selection of unusual foliage. Here, trailing berried laurel adorns a cluster of cineraria, holly, ivy and laurel leaves.

BERRIED LAUREL trails down from the buttonhole

GERBERA AND IVY
A single, deep crimson gerbera is backed by a large, variegated ivy leaf. Such a bold, simple buttonhole forms an immediate, eye-catching "brooch".

MIDSUMMER HEAD-DRESS

I HAVE CHOSEN DELICATE, SWEET-SCENTED FLOWERS in shades of purple and pink to adorn this romantic, traditional head-dress, ideal for a summer wedding. Individually wired and bound flowers and foliage are attached to the main band with gutta-percha tape. The main band is made of two long stub wires, also bound with gutta-percha tape, about 5cm (2in) longer than the circumference of the wearer's head.

MATERIALS AND EQUIPMENT

Head-dresses should be kept light, so you should remove stems and excess foliage and choose fine rose wires and gutta-percha tape.

Flowers and foliage

25 single variegated ivy leaves

6 sprigs of purple lilac

10 purple freesias

6 pink roses

6 guelder roses

Equipment

2 stub wires, 35cm (14in) long, 90 gauge

60 rose wires, 15cm (6in) long, 30 gauge

Roll of gutta-percha tape

VARIEGATED IVY LEAVES weave through the flowers from side to side

DEEPLY SCENTED LILAC and roses are perfect flowers for a head-dress

ANGLE THE FLOWER HEADS to alternate from side to side

MAKING THE HEAD-DRESS

Wire and bind all the flowers and foliage (see pages 178–180) before starting to work.

1 For the main band, overlap the 90-gauge stub wires by 2cm (¾in) and bind them together with tape. Then, starting 2.5cm (1in) from one end, bind two wired ivy leaves to the left side with the tape. Attach a wired lilac sprig to the other side, then an ivy leaf. Add a freesia to the left side, and a rose to the right. Add an ivy leaf and a guelder rose to the left.

THE MAIN BAND is made by binding two stub wires together

ADD THE SAME NUMBER of leaves and flowers in each of the six sections

THE FINISHED EFFECT

The alternating angles of the flowers and ivy ensure the even distribution of colour and shapes along the band. The head-dress can be made one day in advance. Keep it fresh by spraying with water and covering with damp tissue paper in a cool place.

LIME-GREEN GUELDER ROSES contrast with the ivy and complement the light pink roses

SPLIT THE TAPE down its length to make it narrower and lighter

THE SEQUENCE REPEATS on each side of the band, starting with two ivy leaves

Viewed from the back

Side view

2 Beginning on the right side, add two ivy leaves, then the wired flowers and ivy in the same order as step 1. Repeat a further four times, starting each sequence on a different side from the previous one. Finally, bend the band around the head and twist the ends together.

SHOWER BOUQUET

A SHOWER BOUQUET for a wedding is probably one of the most intricate and time-consuming arrangements you will ever make. This breath-taking bouquet is quite complicated to construct, and you should only attempt the project once you have completely mastered the techniques of wiring flowers individually and in units (see pages 177–181). Your effort will be well rewarded.

MATERIALS AND EQUIPMENT

Blooms must be absolutely fresh – remove flowers and foliage direct from potted plants, if possible.

Flowers and foliage

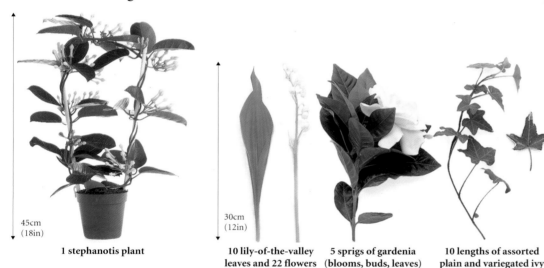

60cm
(24in)

30cm (12in)

DESIGN TIP
The bouquet forms two triangles, one pointing up, the other, twice as long, pointing down. The "return", the top part of the bouquet, forms the upper triangle, and the trail forms the longer lower triangle.

45cm
(18in)

1 stephanotis plant

30cm
(12in)

10 lily-of-the-valley leaves and 22 flowers

5 sprigs of gardenia (blooms, buds, leaves)

10 lengths of assorted plain and variegated ivy

25cm
(10in)

10 stems of white heather

2 cineraria sprigs and 18 single leaves

12 white roses, with leaves

Equipment

50 stub wires, 30cm (12in) long, 70 gauge

120 rose wires, 17.5cm (7in) long, 30 gauge

Reel of fine wire

Roll of gutta-percha tape

2m (6½ft) satin ribbon, 2.5cm (1in) wide

THE FINISHED EFFECT
The colourway is limited to whites, creams and greens, creating a traditional, delicate impression that would complement a wide variety of wedding dresses.

VOLUPTUOUS, creamy roses create a romantic mood

SNOWY GARDENIAS exude a deep, delicious scent

DELICATE LILY-OF-THE-VALLEY bells enhance the feminine tone

TRAILING IVY contributes to the classical associations

BOUQUET HANDLE
The covered wired stems are bound with satin ribbon (see page 183), and decorated with a double bow (see page 182).

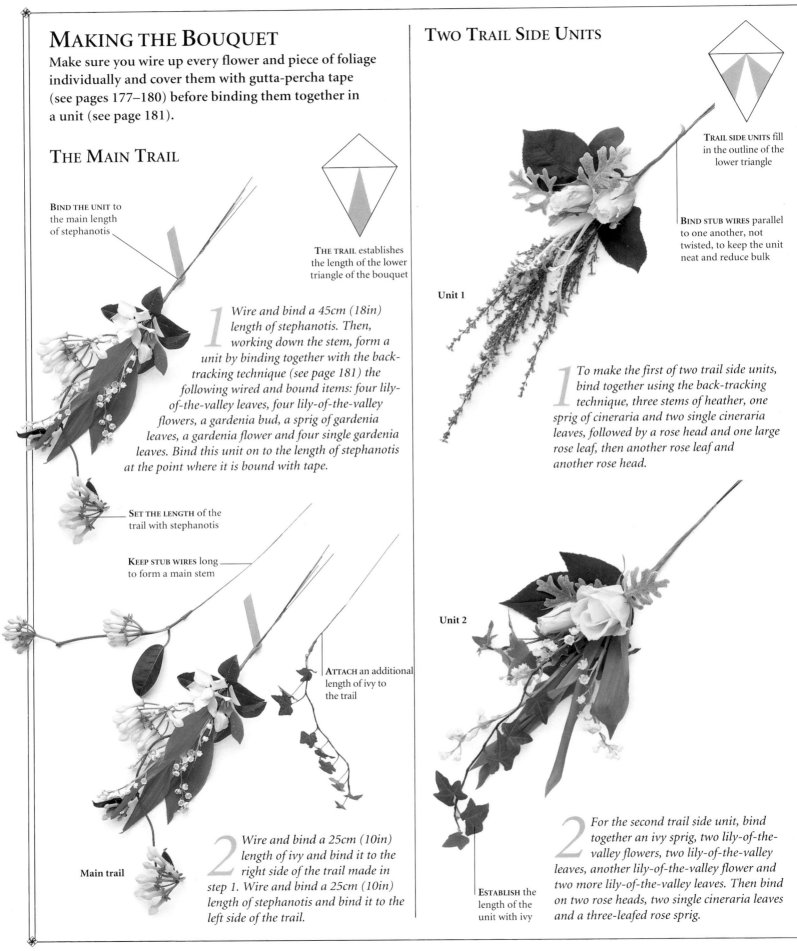

MAKING THE BOUQUET

Make sure you wire up every flower and piece of foliage individually and cover them with gutta-percha tape (see pages 177–180) before binding them together in a unit (see page 181).

THE MAIN TRAIL

BIND THE UNIT to the main length of stephanotis

THE TRAIL establishes the length of the lower triangle of the bouquet

1 *Wire and bind a 45cm (18in) length of stephanotis. Then, working down the stem, form a unit by binding together with the back-tracking technique (see page 181) the following wired and bound items: four lily-of-the-valley leaves, four lily-of-the-valley flowers, a gardenia bud, a sprig of gardenia leaves, a gardenia flower and four single gardenia leaves. Bind this unit on to the length of stephanotis at the point where it is bound with tape.*

SET THE LENGTH of the trail with stephanotis

KEEP STUB WIRES long to form a main stem

ATTACH an additional length of ivy to the trail

Main trail

2 *Wire and bind a 25cm (10in) length of ivy and bind it to the right side of the trail made in step 1. Wire and bind a 25cm (10in) length of stephanotis and bind it to the left side of the trail.*

TWO TRAIL SIDE UNITS

TRAIL SIDE UNITS fill in the outline of the lower triangle

BIND STUB WIRES parallel to one another, not twisted, to keep the unit neat and reduce bulk

Unit 1

1 *To make the first of two trail side units, bind together using the back-tracking technique, three stems of heather, one sprig of cineraria and two single cineraria leaves, followed by a rose head and one large rose leaf, then another rose leaf and another rose head.*

Unit 2

ESTABLISH the length of the unit with ivy

2 *For the second trail side unit, bind together an ivy sprig, two lily-of-the-valley flowers, two lily-of-the-valley leaves, another lily-of-the-valley flower and two more lily-of-the-valley leaves. Then bind on two rose heads, two single cineraria leaves and a three-leafed rose sprig.*

Bound gardenia head and three gardenia leaves

Bound ivy

Top of main trail

Unit 1

ATTACH the first side unit to the left of the main trail

ATTACH the second unit to the right of the main trail

Unit 2

BIND THE IVY to the left of the join

3 Bind the first trail side unit to the left of the main trail and attach the second side unit to the right. Then bind together a gardenia head and three gardenia leaves, and wire and bind a length of ivy.

4 Bind on the gardenia bunch, then the ivy so that the gardenia head lies on the top point of the main trail, and the ivy extends from the left side.

Side view of main trail

BEND THE STEMS back sharply at the join

5 Bend back all the bound stems just below the last sprig of ivy. Make a sharp angle, so that the stems lie almost parallel to the flowers and foliage.

THE RETURN

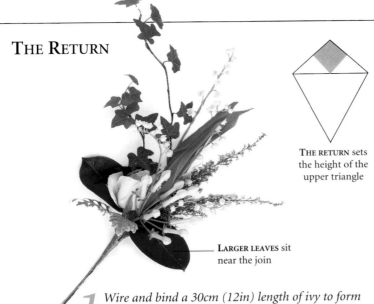

THE RETURN sets
the height of the
upper triangle

LARGER LEAVES sit
near the join

1 Wire and bind a 30cm (12in) length of ivy to form
the main length of the return. Then bind on, using
the back-tracking technique, a lily-of-the-valley
flower, another length of ivy and two ivy leaves, three
lily-of-the-valley flowers, one stephanotis leaf, one rose
head, another large stephanotis leaf and one stephanotis flower
head. Finally, bind on two stems of heather and two cineraria leaves.

BEND THE RETURN
to arch backward

BIND THE STEMS of the
return and trail parallel
to each other

Main trail

2 Hold the bound stems
of the return against the
stems of the main trail so
that the joins of both sets of stems
are close together. Keeping the
stems of both units vertical, bind
them together with tape, about
1cm (½in) down from the join on
each unit. Then bend back the
return to follow the arched line
of the main trail.

THE CENTRE POSY

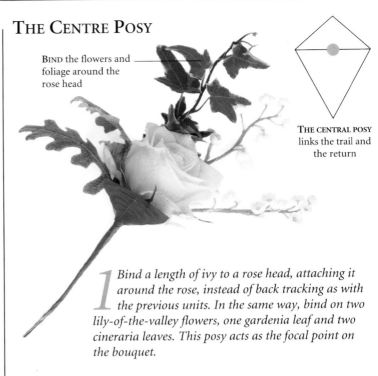

BIND the flowers and
foliage around the
rose head

THE CENTRAL POSY
links the trail and
the return

1 Bind a length of ivy to a rose head, attaching it
around the rose, instead of back tracking as with
the previous units. In the same way, bind on two
lily-of-the-valley flowers, one gardenia leaf and two
cineraria leaves. This posy acts as the focal point on
the bouquet.

Return

ATTACH THE POSY between
the trail and the return

Main trail

2 To attach the posy to the
trail and return, hold its
stems parallel to one side
of the main stem. Make sure the
main flower heads on the posy
extend about 5cm (2in) from the
join of the trail and return,
standing proud of the other
flowers. Bind the posy to the
main stem.

TWO MAIN SIDE UNITS

Unit 1

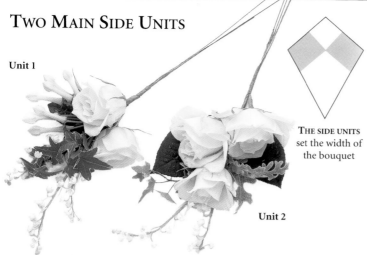

Unit 2

THE SIDE UNITS set the width of the bouquet

1 For the first unit, use the back-tracking technique to bind three lily-of-the-valley flowers, a gardenia leaf, one stephanotis flower and two rose heads to two lengths of ivy. Then make a second unit, the same size as the first. Bind a length of ivy to two lily-of-the-valley flowers, followed by a cineraria leaf, one rose head, one rose leaf, another rose head, a rose leaf and finally a rose head.

FILLER UNITS

Unit 1   **Unit 2**   **Unit 3**   **Unit 4**   **Units 5 and 6**

FILLER UNITS fill out the triangular outlines

1 Make the final six filler units by wiring and binding together the following elements: Unit 1: two stephanotis flower heads; Unit 2: three heather stems and six small cineraria leaves; Unit 3: one lily-of-the-valley leaf, three lily-of-the-valley flowers, two small ivy sprigs and one cineraria leaf; Unit 4: two heather stems, one cineraria sprig and one large cineraria leaf. Make units 5 and 6 from one gardenia flower and three gardenia leaves each.

ATTACH UNIT 2 to the right of the posy

ATTACH UNIT 1 to the left of the posy

2 Hold the first main side unit against the main central stem, to the left of the posy, and bind it on parallel to the other bound stems. Attach the second unit to the right side in the same way.

ATTACH UNIT 5 so that it lies diagonally opposite unit 6

2 Attach the six filler units, as shown, between the return and side units, and between the trail and side units. Finally, bind the handle stems with ribbon and make a bow (see pages 182 and 183).

105

THANKSGIVING DISPLAY

CELEBRATE THE SEASON OF BOUNTIFUL PRODUCE with a lavish basket display that combines vegetables, flowers and foliage. Blocks of dry foam are used to support the pumpkins, while the flowers and foliage are pushed into wet florist's foam. This keeps the vegetables grouped together on one side, with the fresh flowers and foliage on the other, following the principle of grouping ingredients by type.

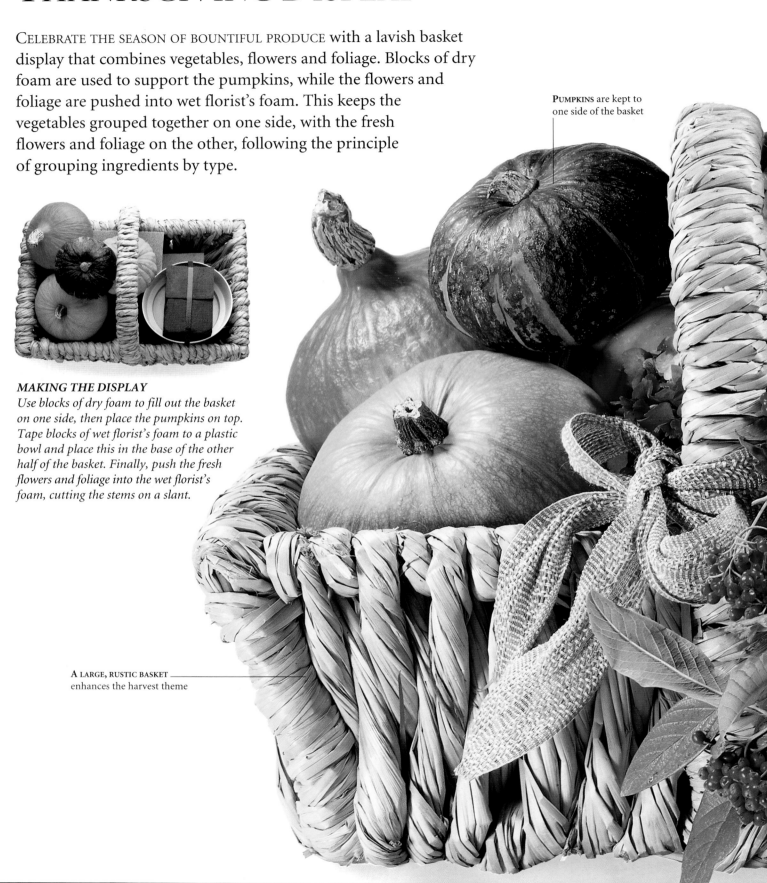

PUMPKINS are kept to one side of the basket

MAKING THE DISPLAY

Use blocks of dry foam to fill out the basket on one side, then place the pumpkins on top. Tape blocks of wet florist's foam to a plastic bowl and place this in the base of the other half of the basket. Finally, push the fresh flowers and foliage into the wet florist's foam, cutting the stems on a slant.

A LARGE, RUSTIC BASKET enhances the harvest theme

SMALL, DELICATE HELENIUM lighten the heavier shapes

MOP-HEADED HYDRANGEAS fill out the display as recessionary flowers

FIERY ORANGE RED HOT POKERS pick up and enhance the orange pumpkins

A CRINKLED, BROWNING LEAF anticipates the onset of autumn

HARVEST DECORATION

FRUIT AND FOLIAGE in the deep russets, reds and browns of autumn are ideal for harvest arrangements. Here, a large weathered terracotta pot has been piled high with smaller terracotta pots, secured with sticks to wet florist's foam. Shiny horse chestnuts, pink heather and cotoneaster berries fill the pots, while grapes tumble over the edge, accompanied by gleaming red apples. Trailing lengths of berried ivy entwine with more pots, apples, grapes and horse chestnuts strewn around the central pot to enhance the impression of opulence.

MAKING THE DECORATION
Line the large terracotta pot with plastic sheeting and fill with blocks of wet florist's foam. Angle the smaller pots to face in different directions, and secure them to the foam with sticks pushed through their drainage holes.

SMALL POTS are secured with sticks pushed through their base into the foam

LENGTHS OF BERRIED COTONEASTER lean out, linking the main pot with the materials lying around it

IVY extends the width of the display and continues the impression of ingredients tumbling out of the pot

SMALL POTS lie casually by the side of the larger one, completing the autumnal composition

STRONG, BUSHY SEDUM
is pushed into wet foam
within the large pot

SHINY RED APPLES are
attached to the foam
with large hairpin hooks

TRADITIONAL CHRISTMAS WREATH

USING A VARIETY of natural festive decorations, this Christmas wreath is simple to make, yet highly effective. The secret is to keep the look simple and avoid crowding on too many decorations. Be selective in your choice of materials and, before starting, plan carefully how to combine and place them. The pine used here will last for around one month.

42cm (17in)

42cm (17in)

DESIGN TIP
The clusters of cones and seed pods create a triangular formation. Likewise, the large red bow is balanced by the bunches of cinnamon wrapped in the same ribbon, forming an opposing triangular shape.

MATERIALS AND EQUIPMENT

Cinnamon sticks are wired in threes, then bound in red ribbon. The other decorations are also wired ready to attach to the wreath (see page 177).

THE FINISHED EFFECT
A rich, traditional and festive Christmas wreath. Selective use of attractive natural decorations, combined with the rich wine-red ribbon, creates a welcoming seasonal door display.

Foliage and decoration

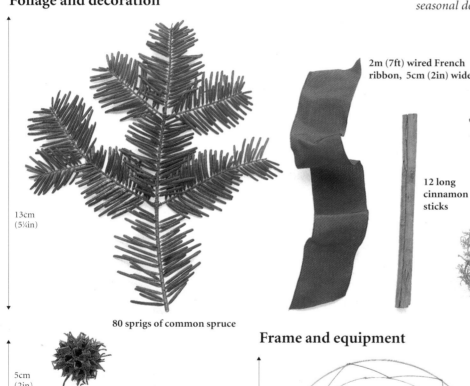

13cm (5¼in)

80 sprigs of common spruce

2m (7ft) wired French ribbon, 5cm (2in) wide

12 long cinnamon sticks

6 pine cones

3 handfuls of lichen moss

CINNAMON STICKS, bound into groups of three with a stub wire, add colour and scent

5cm (2in)

6 round seed pods

Frame and equipment

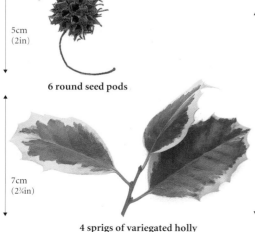

7cm (2¾in)

4 sprigs of variegated holly

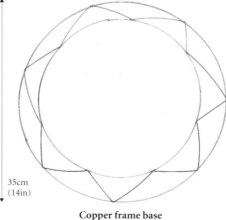

35cm (14in)

Copper frame base

Roll of green string

1 bucket of sphagnum moss

Roll of wreath wrap

140 stub wires, 30cm (12in) long, 90 gauge

GROUPS OF DECORATIONS are equally spaced

CONES are individually wired and grouped closely together in threes, leaving no gaps between

LENGTHS OF RED RIBBON conceal the wire binding and match the bow

LICHEN MOSS is not only a filler, but adds silver highlights

VARIEGATED HOLLY SPRIGS impart extra colour and shine

MAKING THE WREATH

Sphagnum moss is bound to a copper frame with string, and stub wires are used to attach wired spruce and decorations (see page 177). Save the most attractive sprigs for the top of the wreath.

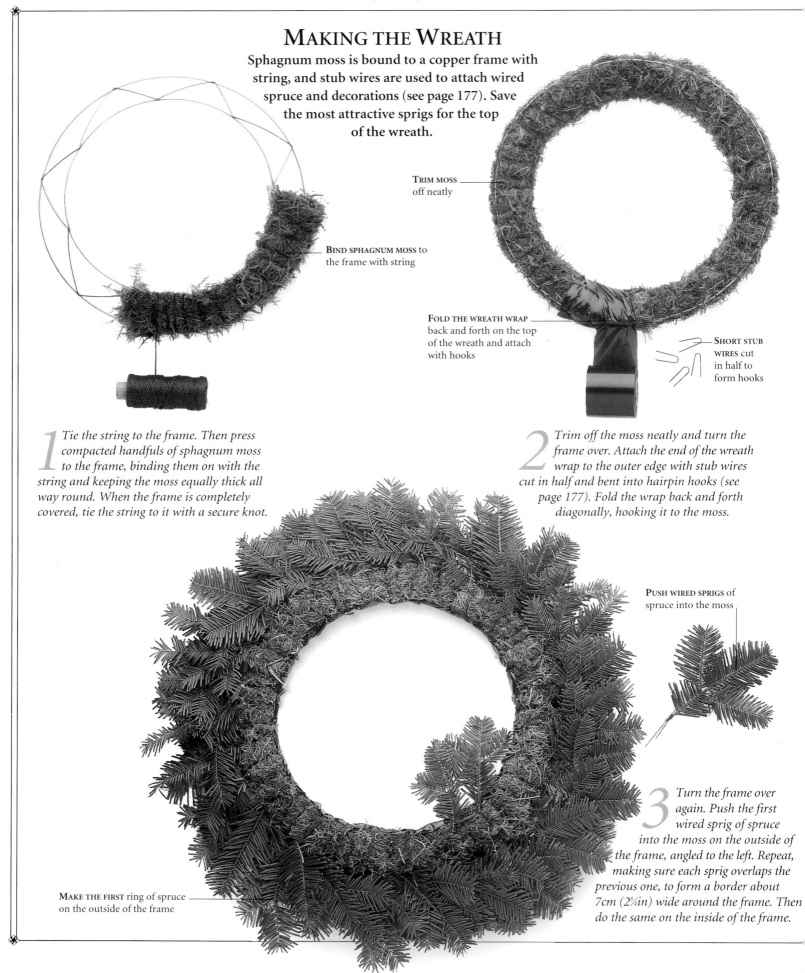

TRIM MOSS off neatly

BIND SPHAGNUM MOSS to the frame with string

FOLD THE WREATH WRAP back and forth on the top of the wreath and attach with hooks

SHORT STUB WIRES cut in half to form hooks

1 *Tie the string to the frame. Then press compacted handfuls of sphagnum moss to the frame, binding them on with the string and keeping the moss equally thick all way round. When the frame is completely covered, tie the string to it with a secure knot.*

2 *Trim off the moss neatly and turn the frame over. Attach the end of the wreath wrap to the outer edge with stub wires cut in half and bent into hairpin hooks (see page 177). Fold the wrap back and forth diagonally, hooking it to the moss.*

PUSH WIRED SPRIGS of spruce into the moss

MAKE THE FIRST ring of spruce on the outside of the frame

3 *Turn the frame over again. Push the first wired sprig of spruce into the moss on the outside of the frame, angled to the left. Repeat, making sure each sprig overlaps the previous one, to form a border about 7cm (2¾in) wide around the frame. Then do the same on the inside of the frame.*

LAY THE TOP ROW of sprigs between the outer and inner rows

THE WIRE binding the cinnamon sticks is concealed with red ribbon

4 Add the most attractive spruce sprigs to the centre of the wreath, to cover the remaining visible moss. Overlap the sprigs in the same direction as the others. Then make a double bow (see page 182) with the wired French ribbon.

5 Attach the bow using a double leg mount (see page 177). Finally, attach two groups of cinnamon sticks bound with red ribbon to create a triangular formation with the bow. Group the other decorations between these points, as shown.

Alternative Colourway

The moss-covered frame forms a base that you can decorate with practically anything you wish. Here, for a very different effect, yet just as festive, the base has been covered with sprigs of holly and decorated with gold-painted globe artichokes and a large green and gold bow.

Alternative foliage and decoration

20 bushy sprigs of holly

4 gold-painted globe artichokes

1m (3¼ft) green and gold wired French ribbon, 10cm (4in) wide

GREEN AND GOLD WREATH
The dark green and gold colours complement each other perfectly. Painted globe artichokes stand out starkly from the base of dark, waxy holly leaves, enriched by the sumptuous green and gold ribbon.

HOLLY SPRIGS replace the spruce

FESTIVE FRUIT SWAG

EXTRAVAGANT AND OPULENT, this swag, embellished with a sumptuous selection of foliage and fruit, makes a perfect Christmas display. I have used ruffled russet silk to enhance the rich reds and browns of the dates, plums, grapes and pears, to create an effect of imperial grandeur.

MATERIALS AND EQUIPMENT
Foliage and decoration

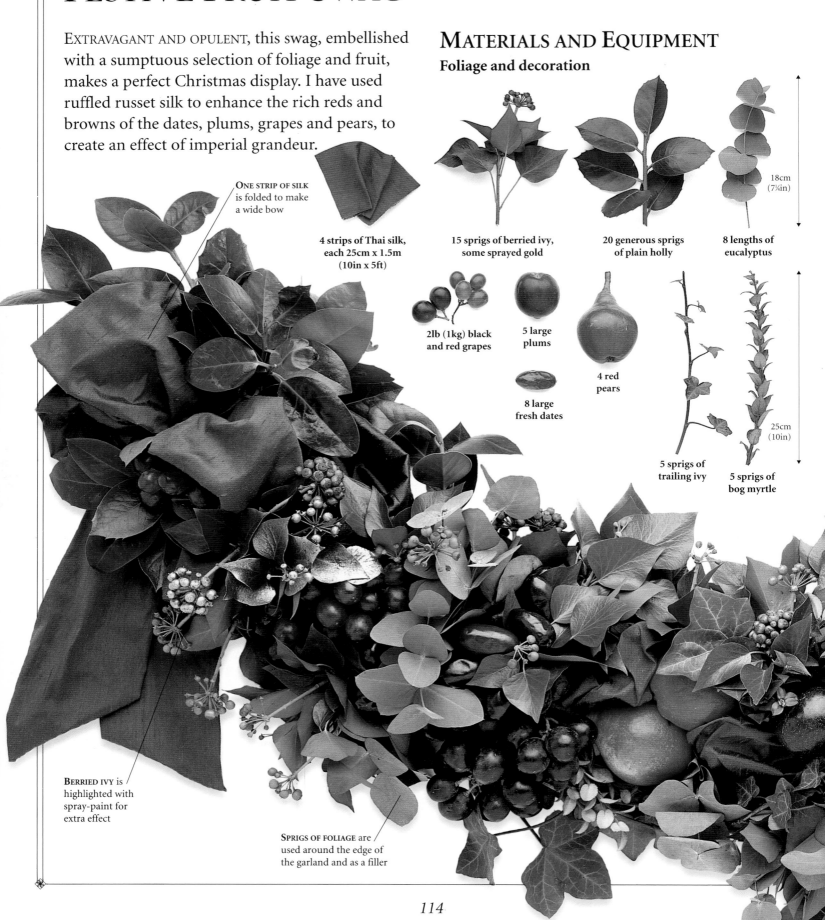

ONE STRIP OF SILK is folded to make a wide bow

4 strips of Thai silk, each 25cm x 1.5m (10in x 5ft)

15 sprigs of berried ivy, some sprayed gold

20 generous sprigs of plain holly

8 lengths of eucalyptus

18cm (7¼in)

2lb (1kg) black and red grapes

5 large plums

4 red pears

8 large fresh dates

25cm (10in)

5 sprigs of trailing ivy

5 sprigs of bog myrtle

BERRIED IVY is highlighted with spray-paint for extra effect

SPRIGS OF FOLIAGE are used around the edge of the garland and as a filler

114

MAKING THE SWAG

Sandwich sphagnum moss between chicken wire to form a band. Gather two lengths of silk and attach along the band with long stub wires formed into hairpin hooks (see page 177). Then make bows with the remaining silk (see page 182) and attach to each end. Wire the foliage and fruit (see page 177) and attach to the band.

Fold chicken wire around the moss to create the base band

ATTACH FRUIT AND FOLIAGE by working from one end of the band to the other

PIN RUFFLED SILK to the moss and wire band with hairpin hooks before adding foliage

GROUP FRUIT by type along the length of the swag

Equipment

Chicken wire, 35cm x 1.5m (14in x 5ft)

3 buckets of sphagnum moss

100 stub wires, 35cm (14in) long, 90 gauge

THE FINISHED SWAG

The richness of the fabric, fruit and foliage can be displayed to best effect if the swag is suspended from a prominent mantelpiece. Use butcher's hooks to hang up the swag, hooked into the wire and moss behind each bow.

FRAGRANT RED PEARS are attached with wires to the middle of the garland for lighter colour contrast

1.5m (5ft)